Martin Nicholas Kunz

best | designed

wellness hotels

INDIA . FAR EAST . AUSTRALIA . SOUTH PACIFIC

avedition lebensart

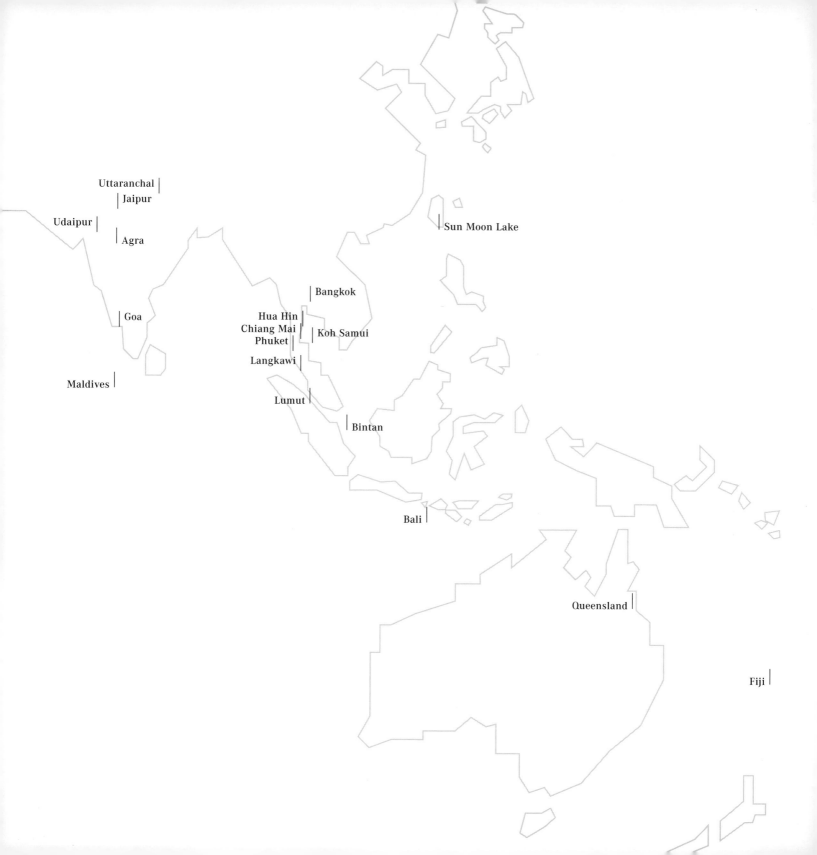

Uttaranchal |

| Jaipur

Udaipur |

| Agra

| Goa

Maldives |

Sun Moon Lake

| Bangkok

Hua Hin |
Chiang Mai |
Phuket |

| Koh Samui

Langkawi |

Lumut |

| Bintan

Bali |

Queensland |

Fiji |

01 | 02

Your head is gently supported by plump upholstery. You gaze down through the hole in the couch at the shimmering green tiled floor, which is spotlessly clean. A faint, pungent cleaning fluid smell penetrates your nostrils – no question about it, no lack of hygiene here. Amazing, the force with which the dainty young woman pinpoints just the right meridian in the sole of your foot. The pain is intense, yet simultaneously a delicious feeling of relaxation spreads through the whole of your body. The aroma of the massage oil begins to suppress the cleaning fluid, your pupils narrow, and you see the green shimmering tiles merge into a dense tropical forest as if from a hang-glider.

The delicate female hands feel like a chunky rolling pin, kneading your back with alternating sweeping movements and well-directed pressure. The skin's sense receptors start to go into overdrive, sending nerve impulses to the brain with lightning speed. The therapist's dexterity visibly relaxes any tense muscles, as your consciousness sails ever more deeply into a tropical green daydream. Piano music interspersed with birds twittering and the sound of a gently rushing stream gradually transforms the enormous treetops, the vines, mammoth ferns and plants into slender fir trees, beech groves, paths and lush meadows.

A wonderful world, a state of total relaxation until... "Okay. Time's up!". You open your eyes and plummet back to earth, even though the room is semi-dark, even though a candle has been lit. The shimmering green tiled floor regains its contours and the door comes into view, stained a dark brown, complete with round arch and imitation baroque handle.

03 04

The meticulous stonework pattern on the beige wallpaper leaps into your line of sight.

A great deal more relaxing still is the steam-bath grotto next door; a perfect blend of art and craftsmanship using 15 different materials, 11 different colours, a profusion of rubber plants and a small holly bush. Between the pillars with their slightly messy gold stripes and unconventional capitals, a miniature multi-tiered fountain,

with an angel at the top, is bubbling away. Kitsch paradise. The water splashes gently down the stone, past the lovingly arranged balls of moss. "Recommended by our Feng Shui adviser", says the lady carrying carrot and apple juice over on a tray. "Important for balancing the body's energies. Would you like a mega-power cocktail?".

Meanwhile, the "atmospheric" music has entered into

competition with the splashing of the fountain, the blubbering of the whirlpool and the drone of the whirlpool's pump. These eventually unite in an eccentric collage of sound, whose disharmony is amplified by the internal architecture's myriad colours and shapes. Despite the blissfully warm, coursing water, tension levels are rising. Your ears send short, pinprick impulses to your brain, your optic nerves are transmitting a whirlwind of image sequences,

resulting in your body tensing up again. The dreamlike glider flight from a tropical forest landscape to the lush meadow pastures fades like a fresh film in sunlight. Back to reality, and your feeling of well-being has vanished. Well, that didn't last long…

All this despite an ancient wisdom: "An aesthetic environment improves the mind; an alert mind is balm for the soul; a happy soul keeps

05

06

the body healthy and full of vitality". The Babylonians, the Egyptians, the Chinese and, of course, the Greeks have left behind ample testimonies to the teachings of beauty, to the harmony of proportion and form, material and colour. Even Socrates and Plato, his pupil, theorised about the interaction between beauty and the spirit. According to Plato's metaphysical philosophy, all things on Earth are derived from their non-material existence. When we recognise them, it is our soul remembering ideas it already knows. If humans have the facility of memory, nothing can remain

hidden from them. Thus, for example, all designs for beds arise from a notion they all have in common: a place to sleep on. Once recognised, beauty is contained in everything, through the notion of beauty alone. Beauty is therefore also relative, since one cannot infer the beauty of one thing from that of another. If we pursue Plato's thinking, it is possible to pick out the most beautiful of apes, which it then is, but among its own kind. The ape's beauty is diminished when compared to a human. Exactly the same is true of human beings and gods. Plato concluded that

something is beautiful if it is right, which begs the question: what is right?

The idea of subjectivity gives rise to a second level of relativity, since the assessment of beauty and the intellectual process are also dependent on the visual impressions an observer has accumulated during the course of his physical life. From a metaphysical perspective, this horizon can even extend to the everlasting life of the soul. From this point of view, either everything is purely a matter of taste or is subordinate to a higher system. An "aesthetic" attempt to

interpret Pythagoras's theorem might be easier to understand: "Beauty is the correspondence of all parts to form a pleasing whole. The most beautiful is when the whole is to the larger part what the smaller part is to the larger part. This is the golden ratio, which is the basis of harmony".

Although that sounds rather theoretical, it is mathematically accurate. On closer examination and using a conscious approach, it is possible to understand it in practical, even emotional terms. The way in which the majority of people react to anything, although

07 08

subjective, is similar in many respects: when observing flowers, leaves or a spiral-shaped snail-shell, for example. Their "higher order" exerts an optical attraction. Precisely what impulses are transmitted to the brain by our visual organs has not yet been scientifically researched, but they could be infinite, logical numerical codes.

Although every plant, every living thing and every natural formation is unique, there are surprisingly few basic forms in the microcosm and the macrocosm. These can be expressed in mathematical terms using the "Fibonacci sequence" of spiralling numbers, according to which each number is the sum of the two preceeding numbers. The ratio between the numbers is unique: the ratio of the larger number (8) to the next smallest in the series (5) is the same as the ratio of the sum of both (13 = 8 + 5) to the larger number (8). The ratio 8 : 5 equals 1.6, 13 : 8 equals 1.625 etc. The larger the Fibonacci number, the more exact this unique ratio is, and the closer it comes to the "golden section's" natural constant "phi". The golden section can be used to "divide" distance "c" into two parts, "a" and "b".

Or, expressed as the following equation: a : b = b : c and c = a + b, which can be resolved as distance b = 1.618... · a or b = φ · a. Today, this is still our best way of explaining harmony. Although Leonardo of Pisa, as Fibonacci was known, did not set out his mathematical discoveries – along with Arabic numerical notation – in his hefty, 500-page tome Liber Abaci before the 12th Century, his predecessors, the intellectuals of classical antiquity, were already on the right track to the "golden section", even without sophisticated mathematics.

The Romans too strived to create harmony between mind, body and soul. They were, in effect, the first real wellness fanatics. Imagine men munching grapes, relaxing in the water, while conducting their political gatherings, business discussions and creative workshops. From an ascetic perspective even today, that might seem like a cliché of decadence. But who knows, this cult of bathing might even have been the source of inspiration and power from which the Romans built their empire, early on, at least. In the third century A.D., sanus per aquam – health

through water, or "spa" for short – developed into a serious trend with all its concomitant distortions. Tradition has it that the Caracalla Thermal Baths in Rome (all 140,000 m² of them) were in operation around the clock, and some bathers are said to have stayed in the water until they collapsed or drowned. This indulgent behaviour can hardly have been responsible for the fall of the Roman Empire however, as by the 4th Century the Patriarch of Constantinople had put an end to the fun by issuing a total ban on bathing.

Modern-day spas are by no means an innovative nor a special phenomenon. In the past, they were known as a place people would go for a "cure" - they had more to do with illness and old age than with health and youth. It is small wonder then that it should be "Roman baths" that have become the symbol of the burgeoning demand for relaxation programmes as an antidote to over-stimulation and hectic everyday life, a Fountain of Youth for the stressed office worker. But it is always easy to lose the sense of perspective, once a new trend has been born. As was the case with the "organic" concept, those handy words "spa" and "wellness" are now producing some weird and wonderful offshoots. When Dr. Halbert Dunn fused the closely related concepts of "well-being" and "fitness" into the word "wellness" during the 1960's, as an expression for his holistic approach to vitality and the prevention of illness, he probably had not the slightest inkling that, decades later, almost every self-respecting country inn with a shabby sauna in the cellar would mutate overnight into a "wellness centre". Ready-made concepts do, of course, run the risk of meaning everything and nothing.

It is not least for that reason that the authors of this book wish to emphasise the inalienable link between aesthetics and everything connected with spas and wellness – ultimately, with health also. Their thesis is, "True balance between body, mind and soul is only to be found in an aesthetic environment".

The benefits of a perfect massage in a tacky treatment room dissipate just as quickly as those of a sauna in a swanky establishment with dubious decor. By contrast, burying yourself in a good

book on your lounger on Vatulele is just as much a part of an active wellness programme as diving off Lizard Island or walking through the paddy fields that surround Ubud on Bali. Or you could sunbathe on the terrace of the Lalu at Sun Moon Lake in Taiwan, be introduced to Tai Chi at the Evason Phuket or enjoy a legendary Martini at Hari's Bar at the Nilaya Hermitage.

And then there is the Fusion Dinner at the Datai on Langkawi or stargazing from the wooden sun deck at Soneva Gili...

01 | Asian relaxation bath, with flowers, fine essences, in the open air.

02 | Harmony between nature and architecture.

03 | Jungle pool at the Banyan Tree, Bintan.

04 | Entrance to the "Clear Water" residence at the Begawan Giri Estate, Bali.

05 | Corridor in the Four Seasons Resort Bali at Sayan.

06 | Obligatory: an open-air shower.

07 | Plant arrangement in the Lana Spa, Regent Chiang Mai, Thailand.

08 | The details make the difference while bathing.

09 | Massage in an aesthetic environment to promote balance between body, spirit and soul

10 | Minimalistic bathing room at The Lalu, Sun Moon Lake, Taiwan.

11 | Inspiration for the senses in pure nature.

12 | Swimming pool in the rainforest. Begawan Giri Estate, Bali.

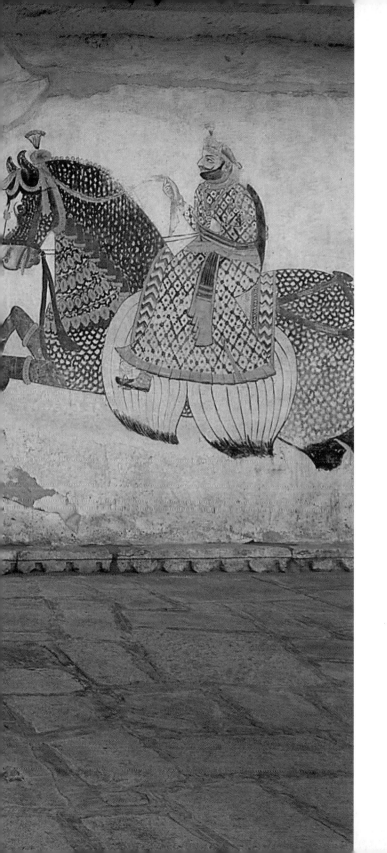

india

amarvilas | agra . india

DESIGN: Benseley Design Studio, Bangkok

The Amarvilas is in one of India's most interesting regions, in the golden triangle between Delhi, Jaipur and Agra. Its heyday was in the 16th and 17th Centuries when the region was ruled by the Moghul dynasty. The most significant examples of the region's architectural heritage, including what is undoubtedly the most famous building in India, the Taj Mahal, date from this era. The Taj Mahal was built in the mid-17th Century by ruling Moghul Emperor, Shah Jahan, as a mausoleum to his favourite wife, Mumtaz Mahal. The vast marble monument, which took 20,000 men 22 years to build, consumed enormous amounts of money and labour, and took the Shah Jahan to the brink of financial ruin.

Managed by Oberoi, the Amarvilas opened at the beginning of 2001. Almost within touching distance of the Taj Mahal, it is the only hotel which directly overlooks the monument. In the shadow, as it were, of the magnificent building opposite that attracts millions of tourists every year, the Amarvilas offers guests an uninterrupted view of the memorial from every one of its 112 rooms. One of the privileges of staying at this luxury resort is to be able to experience the imposing sight as the light changes during the course of the day. However, the hotel's close relationship with its illustrious neighbour finds expression in more than the fact that virtually every part of the hotel looks out onto the Taj Mahal; indeed, the whole complex radiates an altogether more profound, all-penetrating attachment to the model that inspired it.

In order to achieve this, the architects have not merely sought to reflect the essence of the Taj in the formal language of the new building but also in their choice and treatment of internal and external materials. For example, the architectural features in the entrance area – the marble pools, fountains, stone balustrades and plants – all bear traces of the Taj Mahal and its design. Above all, the planners have taken care to use traditional craftsmanship on the finished surfaces that give definition to the hotel's spaces. This has meant consciously avoiding recent techniques in favour of creating the kind of authentic atmosphere that can only be achieved with genuine, living craftwork. One of the most famous techniques of ornamentation used here is known as "pietra dura" - the same Florentine stone inlaying technique that embellishes the walls of the rulers' graves in the Taj. The sumptuously appointed rooms at the Amarvilas – the Kohinoor Suite in particular – have teak surfaces, fine silks and chandeliers of hand-blown crystal, and radiate an ambience of pure luxury.

Other impressive aspects of the Amarvilas are the unparalleled levels of comfort and countless special touches its well-heeled guests can expect. It has two restaurants, a bar and a handsome domed lounge serving an infinite diversity of delectable Asian and continental cuisine. The leisure area also offers plenty of variety and features mostly traditional Indian treatments, including Ayurveda, steam baths, massage treatments and aromatherapy.

01 | Opened in 2001, despite the Amarvilas' historical look, the
construction never slips into kitsch.

02 | The hotel's architecture is drawn from Indian palaces, although the
reduction of decoration provides a contemporary interpretation of
luxury. With 112 rooms, the property still manages a certain
exclusivity.

It's not found in any guidebooks, it doesn't advertise, and without a local driver, it's nearly impossible to find. Well hidden and accessible by small, narrow roads, this rustic retreat lies on a thickly forested hill, a good hour's drive from the airport at Goa. Such are the ideal prerequisites for a secret resort comfortably removed from nearby tourist centres, crowded beaches, sun burnt package tourists and non-stop rave parties.

Along with backpackers and hippies, Goa is now a favourite of Britpoppers and Ibiza-styled party-types looking for their next tropical hot spot. In other words, this 3700 km^2 province with its many kilometres of palm-lined, sandy beaches is celebrating a new-found popularity. Unlike other mass tourism locales, Goa's hype is confined to a few compact enclaves. Even with its hordes, paradise can still be found just a few miles from the scene-makers. And Nilaya – which means "heaven" in Sanskrit – is indeed one such paradise, located beyond the packs of cows, dogs and carefree cyclists lining Goa's main roads, safely in the hills of Apora, where time seems to flow on a different schedule.

Panoramic views across a palm forest out to the Arabian Sea, gently soothing fragrant winds, comfortable lounge chairs and indulgent inaction – these are Nilaya's greatest offerings, tempered only by an Ayurvedic massage centre, fine cuisine and refreshing cocktail conversation.

And there are ample opportunities for conversation and contact at the Nilaya Hermitage. Although the resort's spacious guest quarters are an ideal spot for solitude, guests tend to congregate round the pool. This makes sense considering the pool's beauty, but take a look at the hotel's guest book and these visitors are the types more associated with well-guarded holiday compounds than an easy-going, yet luxurious retreat. But it is squarely because of the Nilaya's uncomplicated charm that the hotel has become the travel topic of conversation within the global arts crowd who return to the resort time and time again. Whether a London lighting designer, an Australian PR boss, a German musician or a Swedish star photographer, at the pool or in the nearby bar area, guests happily hop from

01 | The pool is a centre-point for conversation and meeting. In the main building is the open lobby and the music / meditation room.

02 | All rooms, except one, have an open construction.

03 | Lobby.

one bar-stool to another. People get to know each other, business deals are arranged and tales of that day's events begin to be told, until a new dash of excitement grabs everyone's attention. The gripping novel one guest is enjoying suddenly loses its thrill when the resident princess from Dubai makes an entrance. She's here with a crowd of stunning accomplices, one of whom bumps into her ex-boyfriend who doesn't remain ex for long, leaving his own female companion on her own to find new friends among the hotel's eligible bachelors.

Such is the drama that unfolds in this beautiful, magnetic complex. Alongside its peace and serenity, the creativity and zest for life of the Nilaya's owners shines brightly. Claudia Derain and Hari Ajwani met each other in Goa in 1986, and as Hari, an agile Indian engineer who studied in Berlin tells it, "we fell in love". Claudia hails from Cologne, and experienced the world as a diplomat's daughter. Eventually, she wound up in Paris where she worked for designer Thierry Mugler. Together, she and Hari make an energetic couple whose imagination and charisma are authentically

reflected to the smallest detail at Nilaya, where they have made real their take on the ideal hotel. "We wanted to bring aesthetics, pleasure and unobtrusive service together because these elements belong together," says Hari, who will readily speak of the myriad of mediocre hotel experiences which shaped this philosophy.

Doing things better began in 1992 with the purchase of a 65,000 m² parcel of land on a mountainside in Goa. This choice of location went in the face of Goa's traditional touristic lures. "Tourists in Goa

want those beautiful beaches," is the area's conventional wisdom. "But individualists will come to us," thought Hari and Claudia. And this mindset proved correct, as a small, unique retreat eventually proved to be just as much a success as the beachside resorts.

For the couple, doing things better meant, above all, creating an aesthetic steeped in sensuality. With the support of local architect Dean D'Cruz, the group designed a modern-day fairy tale which has managed to draw both guests and respect from traditionally

04

tough architecture critics. Comparing the property is difficult, though it does inspire thoughts of Hundertwasser, only with less ecological kitsch.

Materials from the surrounding area blend with Goan workmanship at Nilaya. The buildings' organic forms and strong colours manage to fit perfectly. Furnishings, fabrics, accessories and lighting complement each other in sinuous harmony. Each hotel view opens up new windows of discovery, evident from the "oohs" and "aahs" they elicit from recent arrivals. There's an art exhibition feel to Nilaya, which often prompts guests to re-think the design of their own homes or offices. Luckily, Claudia and Hari are well aware of this condition, and have recently opened "Sangolda", an interior design and accessories shop offering numerous souvenirs of all sizes at reasonable cost.

04 | This room has an organic cupola form. The terrace doors are made of untreated tin.

05 | Steps along the main building to the terrace restaurant.

06 | Each of the 11 rooms is built differently and is decorated with a mixture of craftwork.

07 | Sun-loungers at the pool. From here, one can gaze across palm trees to the Indian Ocean.

08 | There are almost no windows. Instead, long trains of fabric cover openings in the walls, allowing for comfortable ventilation.

09 | This rooms is dedicated to the theme "Sun", with its gold and yellow tones.

10 | Hari's open-air bar is a legendary meeting point for global creatives.

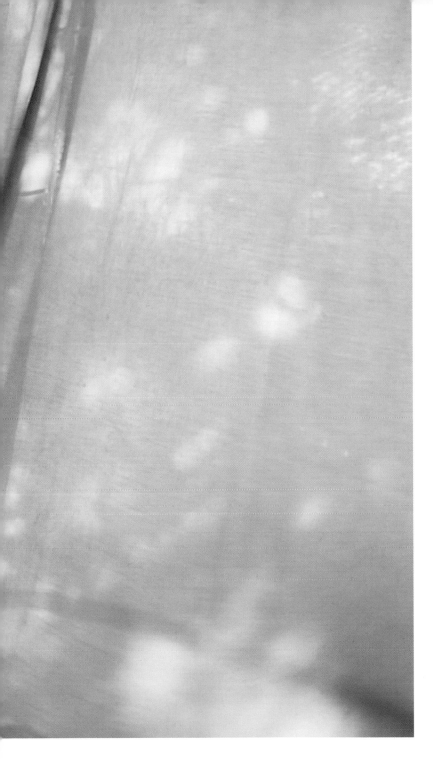

The retreat's 11 guest areas (to simply call them "rooms" would be a monumental understatement), are all different and unique. Each is named after a cosmic element: Sun, moon, stars, water, fire, earth and air. Only one has real windows and is definitely the quarter of choice during the rainy season in summer. The others are more or less open-air in style, either due to holes in their domed roofs for looking at the stars from canopied beds, or through openings in the walls themselves, which are lightly covered in breezy fabrics to allow in the sun's rays.

Some showers offer views to the skies as well, while the bathrooms and toilets are cordoned off from living and sleeping quarters not by doors, but rather via curving, spiraling walls which block out curious peeks. Even the terraces, with their jungle-to-ocean views, allow for peace and privacy despite close proximity to the main building and pool. Another of the Nilaya's unique aspects is its "music dome". Following numerous colour updates, the dome is now blue and boasts walls inlaid with small marble tiles. This cupola-roofed building serves as the resort's meditation HQ, where relaxation transpires according to the moods of the guests, whether in the form of sheer silences, or when transformed into a dance floor for a spontaneous party. Such freedom to do as once chooses, to feel at complete ease, is a crucial component of Nilaya's philosophy. In fact, guests can even eat when and how they choose: Nilaya is one of the few hotels worldwide where breakfast is served 24-hours a day, either in your room, by the pool or on the terrace. And if you want it, we suspect Claudia and Hari's attentive staff would even serve coffee and rolls right on the hotel's tennis court.

01 | Living in royal safari style. The 17 tented suites are among the most popular of the 71 guestrooms.

02 | They are airy, calmly coloured, a little plush but designed without pomp.

03 | View to the fort, with lobby, restaurants and courtyard.

01

02

03

rajvilas | jaipur . india
DESIGN: Benseley Design Studio, Bangkok

On the approach flight to Jaipur one can already recognize its hills covered with castles, forts and palaces. The city in the core of Rajasthan is regarded as a centre of splendid architecture, and not without good reason. The city is abound with richly decorated sights, giving visitors a sense of the tremendous wealth the Indian nobility once enjoyed. Visiting such famous places as the Palace of the Winds (Hawa Mahal), the City Palace, Nahargarh Fort or the Jaigarh Fort is to dive into a completely different world, where western shapes and forms are replaced by dream-like structures, surrounded in mystery and legend. The naked reality of modern India's streets, however, will startle you from such dreams and bring you down to earth with a bump. There can be few other places in the world were radical poverty and fantastic splendor clash so extremely. Those who will not or cannot bear these crass opposites, and adjust to the Indian mindset, should simply not come. Those who manage to pick up some of the Indian people's serenity, composure and, in some respects, fatalistic attitude to the course of life's events will be rewarded with a spiritual, personal experience.

Admittedly an ultramodern hotel in an environment overloaded with decorative elements would be an aethstetic challenge – cool and avant-garde, The Rajvilas is certainly not. Rather than this, P. R. S. Oberoi was inspired by the renovation of an historical fort in nearby Naila, which the family uses as a private residence. The area where the resort is located today was still fallow land just ten years ago, so the hotel's architecture is clearly contemporary. Given the context, however, there was a great danger that an unspectacular tourist block would have developed, characterless, meaningless and standardized. Oberoi, however, wanted something "old-new", mirroring the charm of Rajasthans' heyday.

Out of this, a structure blended from pure imagination and historicism emerged; a solution that may have left many critics of architecture shuddering. The result shows great stylistic harmony though, with decorations that are never exaggerated, a well-balanced colour scheme, and a finely coordinated choice of materials. The trio of planners, consisting of Indian architect, Prabhat Patki, the design office, H. L. Lim & Associates, from Singapore and the

04

05

American landscape designer, Bill Bensley, have clearly succeeded in creating an aesthetic symbiosis well beyond the limitations of Disneyland and Las Vegas.

The limited size of the resort alone lends a maximum of exclusivity to it. The centre is formed by a fortress-like main building with lobby, restaurant and meeting areas. This main building, with its four thick towers, is bordered by a red wall, and the 71 guestrooms are dotted around it. Within the 14-hectare property, these are split up into small residential complexes with four to six luxury rooms, as well as three mansions, each with their own swimming pool. The 17 tent-covered luxury suites are particularly popular, exuding a radiant interior design.

The hotel's wellness facilities enjoy a global reputation. In a centre covering 2000 m^2, embedded in a tropical park with herb garden and a central swimming pool, guests can enjoy a manifold menu of massages and relaxation therapies as well as the almost mandatory saunas, steam bath, jacuzzi and exercise room.

04 | The reception is located in the main building, as well as the restaurants. One of these offers a decorated courtyard and stage for evening events.

05 | Restaurant.

06 | Living room in one of the three pool villas.

07 | Refined camping: covered terrace of a tent suite.

07
08

anánda in the himalayas | uttaranchal tehri garwahl . india

DESIGN: Chhada Siembieda + Associates

Silk saris, snow-covered mountain tops or the holy river – Rishikesh is where many worlds come together. Situated north-east of New Delhi, this Indian town is reputed to be the ultimate place of the holy and wise. The Beatles came to Rishikesh in the '60's seeking closeness to God, inner peace and health. They hoped to experience all this through meditation and the ancient Indian art of nutrition, and it is not without reason that this town at the foot of the

Himalayas is known as the birth place of yoga, Ayurveda and meditation. Those wishing to escape the din of car horns and the turbulent bustle of gurus, wanting to learn about Indian healing arts, will find a pure haven of relaxation only a few kilometres away. The Ananda first opened its doors to the public in September 2000. Ananda, meaning "bliss and self-satisfaction" in Sanskrit, is a welcome contrast to the lively commotion in Rishikesh.

Following its remodelling, the old palace of the Tehri Garhwal maharaja is already reputed among specialists to be one of India's most beautiful wellness resorts. The peaceful oasis extends over roughly 100 hectares. Here ancient Indian traditions are combined with the latest discoveries in Western medicine. Seventy rooms and five suites offer relaxation. The "Valley View" rooms afford magnificent views of the Ganges, whilst guests staying in the "Garden" rooms

as well as in the deluxe and "Rafael" suites have their own private garden. The rooms are furnished with teak-wood furniture, reminiscent of the bygone times of the Raj. Hand-made accessories and tantric art decorate the hallways and hotel rooms. From the panoramic tub in the bathroom, the guests look out onto the Himalayan peaks and the Ganges flowing through the valley. An exquisite scent of sandalwood and exotic flowers lingers everywhere. It is the

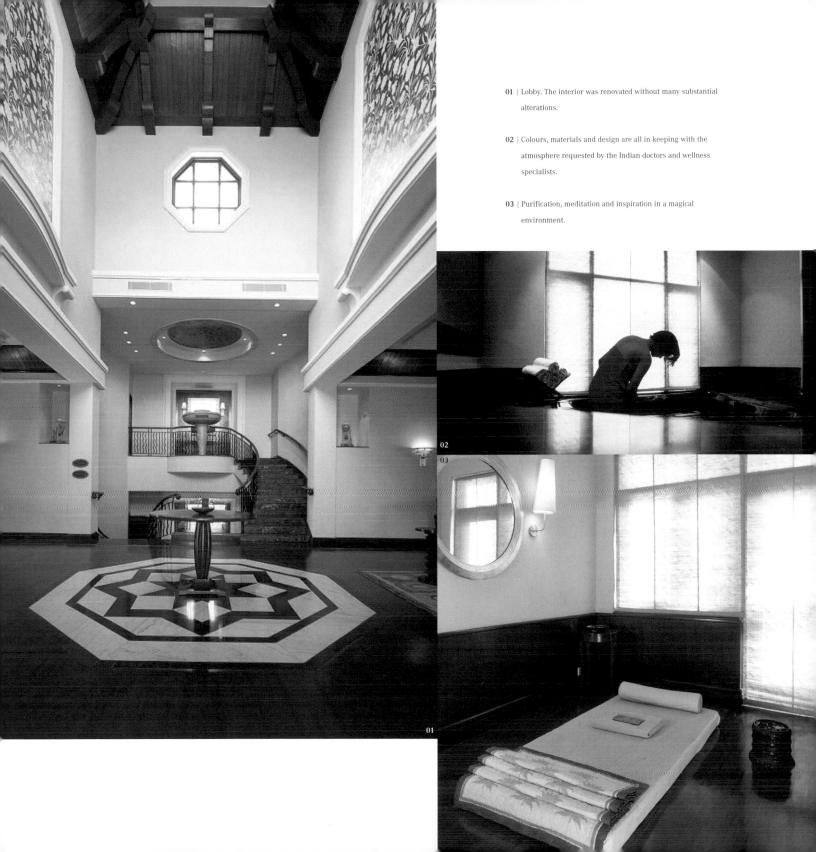

01 | Lobby. The interior was renovated without many substantial alterations.

02 | Colours, materials and design are all in keeping with the atmosphere requested by the Indian doctors and wellness specialists.

03 | Purification, meditation and inspiration in a magical environment.

04

05 06

interesting little peculiarities that give these luxury lodgings their charm. The oldest billiard room in India, for example, is in the Ananda. The tea lounges bear witness to the English influence on the country, and on special occasions a large orchestra plays classical pieces in the ballroom.

Yet for most guests what makes a stay in this house, dating from 1895, unforgettable is the vast array of wellness treatments on offer. Whether it be an anti-jetlag hydromassage in bubbling spring water, facial treatments with Himalayan honey and rose water or the synchronous Ayurveda massage followed by a flower petal bath, this spa resort, covering an area of approximately 2000 m², offers a therapy for everyone. Ayurveda doctors and yoga instructors create individual well-being programmes for the duration of your stay.

East and west are also blended in both of the restaurants. The menu offers international cuisine, and all dishes are enhanced using herbs and vegetables from the hotel's own garden. Although the noble hotel is situated in a holy area, a pre-dinner G and T can still be enjoyed – permission to serve alcoholic drinks had to be sought from no less an authority than the Indian Prime Minister himself. Exploring the surrounding areas is a little easier to arrange. Safaris, kayaking and rafting tours can all be organized by the hotel's efficient staff.

devi garh | udaipur . india

DESIGN: Navin Gupta, Gautam Bhatia, Rajv Saini, Poddar Family

It's a mere 26km in distance and a one-hour drive in the back seat of an Ambassador Classic from Udaipur airport to the unique Indian palace of Devi Garh and its contemporary, minimalist interior architecture. On this short journey into the heart of Rajasthan, it's not only the holy cows and oxen that often get in the way. There are dogs who regularly risk and lose their lives en route, camels swinging along the road's barely visible curbstones and elephants, pigs and apes all adding to the flow of traffic. That's not to mention the jeeps, three-wheelers, rickshaws and numerous hand-carts.

Devi Garh is eventually announced on a prominent road sign, where an arrow pointing right indicates the hotel's entry gate, soon to be opened by a saluting guard. The Ambassador turns onto the dusty track, follows a long curve around a hill and then comes to a complete surprise. Like a mirage, the ochre-yellow palace stands before you. Strategically well positioned on the hill, this 18th-century abode was actually built as a fort and is surrounded by the village of Delwara, which is nearly hidden between the shimmering red-brown Aravali Hills and set on one of the three main travel routes between Udaipur and Jaipur.

In the course of its history the estate continually developed from a protected place of retreat into a filigreed palace until its final sale to the Rajasthani government in the 1960's. Since that time plenty of money and even more enthusiasm have helped rescue the palace from on-going decline. Its owner Lekha Poddar, is from a well-to-do industrial family, and not only saved this showpiece from complete dereliction, but formed one of the most successful symbiosis of historical substance and contemporary architecture from it. Every square centimetre displays the passion Mrs. Poddar invested in the project. In the same way as the ancient Indian nobles turned their dreams into reality – often ignoring financial limitations in the process – Mrs. Poddar has brought her own personal dream of a luxury hotel into the world without the traditional restraint of a businesswoman.

01 | Almost appearing like a mirage, a breathtaking construction. Further down, below the pool level, is the extensive spa and fitness centre, including Ayurveda treatments

02 | The Devi Garh suite and Palace suite share this pool.

It is hard to believe such an enormous estate houses a mere 23 suites. Lekha Poddar lays much of the hotel's value in its exclusivity, almost as if she would prefer to reserve this imposing setting just for her friends and their private parties. To the smallest detail, everything here betrays nothing but the best: from the air-conditioning, perfectly hidden in the stonework, to the silk embroidered cushions, to the water bowls with lotus flowers, to the marble dishes with pistachios and almonds, to the delicate toothbrush glasses and hand-made slippers.

A walk through the complex is like a voyage of discovery. Every step clarifies the intensity with which Poddar and her design team laboured. Chief

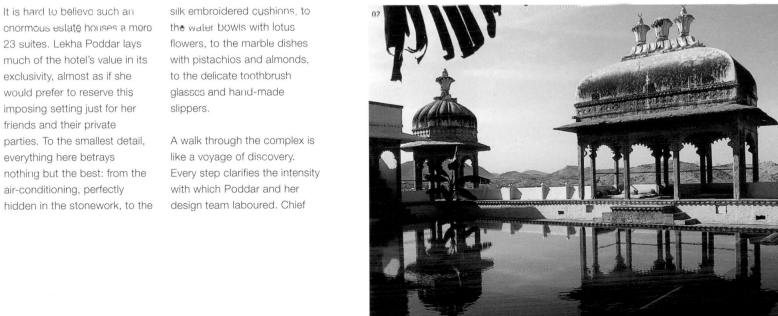

03

among Poddar's crew were Navin Guptar and Gautam Bhatia of The Architecture Alliance, Delhi, along with interior designer Rajiv Saini from Bombay. The group planned and built for more than a decade, paying close attention to architectural and archeological discoveries and never allowing themselves to

destroy the property's historic authenticity.

In contrast to the retreat's richly ornamented, oriental external architecture, the interior design is distinctly minimalist. Innumerable bay windows, towers, canopies, cloisters, bridges, terraces, balconies and courtyards meet

with floors, bed pedestals and custom-made furniture crafted from the highest quality white marble mined from local quarries. Soft furnishings and seating cushions in the overhanging bay windows are woven from the finest linen and form a comfortable seat for viewing the panoramic vistas across the nearby hills.

Meanwhile, dazzling flower motifs and simple ornamentation break the slick whiteness of the minimalist marble floors and smooth, plastered walls. They're the perfect inlay work and a stunning tribute to a centuries old craft interpreted modernly in a novel and luxurious setting.

04

05

03 | A relaxing corner.

04 | In contrast to the building's external decoration, the rooms have a certain mini-
malism.

05 | A place to escape the sun, behind metre-thick protective walls.

indonesia

amankila | bali . indonesia

DESIGN: Edward Tuttle

In Sanskrit, Amankila means "peaceful hill". Here, in just such an environment in Bali's south-east, is a resort near the small ferry port of Padangbai, where ships connect to the islands of Nusa Penida and Lombok. Like a huge temple, the resort sits among heavily forested rocks overlooking a white, private beach.

With only 35 villa-suites – seven of them with private pools – even at full capacity, guests will rarely feel crowded. This is intentional: A sense of exclusivity was the primary goal when creating Amankila.

Along with having one of the loveliest beaches in Bali, the hotel also boasts a pool which other hotels can only hope to compete with. Located in the palm garden beach club, the pool is 150 feet long. Three other swimming pools cascade upon one another in front of the hotel's main restaurant and are perhaps Amankila's most unique architectural feature.

The pools are surrounded by small pavilions with cushioned sun chairs; a more inviting alternative to traditional deck chairs for waterside relaxing. Amankila's villas are built into

the surrounding hillside and each features a furnished terrace with views extending to the sea. Here, a sumptuous breakfast or outstanding meal may be taken in a luxurious, intimate atmosphere.

The interior architecture at Amankila is both functional and decorative. A Balinese flavour may be found in the carved, wooden columns on otherwise staid four-poster beds. Nearby, sliding doors lead to the bath area decorated by profiled wall linings which, perhaps, could have been left out. But to waste time on

such minutiae, here in one of the world's true premier resorts, would be pedantic. Instead, it is better to focus on the aesthetic path and staircase system that interconnects Amankila's buildings, or on the sensitive blending of its building materials and the hotel's many lovely details.

01

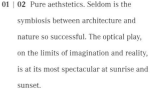

02

01 | 02 Pure aethstetics. Seldom is the
symbiosis between architecture and
nature so successful. The optical play,
on the limits of imagination and reality,
is at its most spectacular at sunrise and
sunset.

03 | The complex has 35 villas; seven of
them with private pool.

03

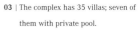

04 | Guests can arrive by car upto the lobby with its lotus flower

canals. Behind here, the way is by foot over walkways and steps.

05 | A typical detail – this time a sign for the WC. Men's or women's?

06 | Each of the villas has a terrace with seaview.

07 | Cool stone floors, local woods and reserved craftwork are characteristic of the interior design.

08 | Light and shadow in the shower. Some of them offer a panoramic view of the ocean.

09

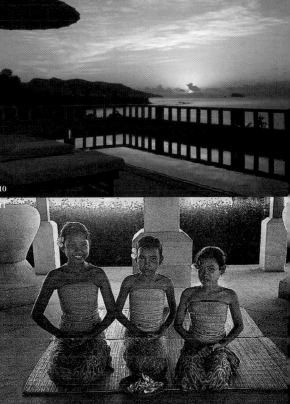

10

11

09 | Pool suite number 34. For most visitors, a stay
here counts among their once-in-a-lifetime
experiences.

10 | It sits atop a cliff, with a breathtaking vista of the
most beautiful fine sand beach on the whole
island, the rocks behind it and the endless ocean.

11 | The crafts and folk arts on display are more
authentic than in the tourist centres.

01 | A small village, with geometric and
minimalist architecture, hides in the
hills behind the Nusa Dua beach.

the balé | bali . indonesia

DESIGN: Anthony Lui Karl Princic

On the peninsula Nusa Dua, near the southernmost part of Bali, some of the island's most luxurious hotels have been established and now advertise their outstanding service. Close to the famous temple of Ulu Watu lies the design resort, The Balé, opened only in the spring of 2002. With just twenty pavillions it guarantees exclusivity and a romantic environment. Even by Balinese standards, with its high density of well-designed hotels, the new resort takes on an exceptional position. As in almost no other case, minimalist design and a strict stylistic idiom dominate at The Balé.

Within the close arrangement of the individual buildings an almost urban structure has been developed. The pavillions form lanes, alleys and courts, in a genuine contrast to other complexes, which meander and take their form from the surrounding tropical nature.

The guest's private sphere is guaranteed despite the close arrangement of the buildings. Each villa has its own enclosed garden, slightly elevated above the public area, making surrounding walls unnecessary. A private, yet pleasantly open impression is the result. The central element of the garden is a long water basin, and it's a joy to experience how finely this garden is arranged. Grass surfaces, stone paths and stone terraces are the components of a balanced whole, glinting with Asiatic simplicity. A bed on one of the shady terraces is a marvellous place for a nap during the day or also at night. One experiences the garden as an extension of the interior, as intended by the planners, which appears only natural with the local climate. The restaurant "Faces" is located next to the main pool. Here Swiss cook, Marcel Huser, combines his international experiences with regional specialties in an open kitchen.

The pavillions are uncompromisingly modern, but respect the culture of Bali. Traditional elements, such as the straw roofs, have been freshly interpreted. In this fashion, a remarkable synthesis between tradition and modern trend, between Asiatic and European elements has developed. The interiors impress by their cool, material elegance, contrasting with a rich culture and the lavishly tropical nature of Bali.

02 | A central element of the guesthouses is an extended water pool that begins directly before the bathroom door and continues to the edge of the garden.

03 | View over the villa's own pool into the bathroom with its glass sliding door.

04 | With 20 spacious pavillion suites, the resort has an exclusive, private atmosphere.

begawan giri estate | bali . indonesia

DESIGN: Cheon Yew Kuan, Terry Fripp, Ratina Huliono, Debbie and Bradley Gardner

Bali's Begawan Giri Estate is a project so grand in scope and imagination that it resulted in not one, but five residences spread throughout a 30-acre property, 20 minutes from the arts colony of Ubud and an hour from the airport at Denpasar. The resort, whose name means "Wise Man's Mountain", is located on a ridge towering over the Ayung River gorge, an area which has developed over the past two decades into a magnet for luxury-loving solitude seekers.

But even in the midst of stunning competing properties, there is no denying the Begawan Giri's innate uniqueness, due mostly to its owners, British expatriates Bradley and Debbie Gardner.

With pasts spent both as bohemians and London-based business-owners, the Gardners had experienced the world and knew what they wanted from it by the time they first visited Bali in the late 1980's. By the end of that stay, what the Gardners wanted was a secluded, luxurious hideaway, high in the Balinese hills – a dream which more than a decade later would emerge as the Begawan Giri Estate.

The resort is first experienced after the short journey along a simple asphalt road linking it to Ubud. Once in the resort, the most distinct feeling is one of agreeable solitude. With a mere 22 suites spread over the resort's five residences, it's possible to see nary another guest during an entire visit.

While all five residences are named after natural elements, share mountainside locales and are designed and decorated to the highest of international standards, their looks and feels are distinct, bearing the results of Malaysian architect Cheong Yew Kuan's eclectic aesthetic influences.

The bi-level Bayugita, or "Windsong", was the first residence to be constructed and is clearly Balinese in design with tell-tale alang-alang roofs and delicate carved wooden detailing. Nearby is Tirta-Ening, or "Clear Water"; a four-bedroom residence defined by three stone and wood structures with a central water pavillion and elegant, lily-filled water gardens. The third residence,

Tejasuara, means "Sound of Fire" and resulted from Gardner's love of architecture and furniture he found in the Indonesian island of Sumba. 1,200 tons of Sumbanese stone were imported to construct the complex, which was balanced with floors crafted of native merbau wood, a protected species so rare that the resort had to source the material from salvaged telephone polls. The most primitive of the residences, Tejasura is comprised of five separate buildings all with thatched roofs and spartan wooden furniture. On the resort's south-east side is Wanakasa, "Forest in the Mist", a five-bedroom villa set on stilts high above verdant vegetation and built around an ancient banyan tree.

01 | Wellness at Begawan Giri is more than just massage. The complex creates an ambiance of inspiration and relaxation through its use of aesthetic and mystic touches.

02 | Approach and lobby of the Tirta-Ening or "Clear Water" residence.

03 | Pool area of the Umbona, "House of the Earth" residence.

And finally, there's Umabona, the "House of the Earth Son", reached by a stone walkway leading to a two-storey teak house filled with formal furnishings such as a hand-carved mahogany dining table.

The residences all have a communal feel, thanks to their central pool and leisure/dining area. Guests looking for absolute peace will certainly find it at the Begawan Giri, though they will bump into fellow visitors if they have not reserved an entire residence. But then again, with expansive rice paddies, tropical forests and a mountain's worth of stone-terraced gardens on site, there's plenty of the Begawan Giri to go around.

04 | Surrounded by rainforest, the almost
suspended granite pool of the "Clear Water"
residence.

05 | Entrance to the open lobby of "Wanakasa". It is
located above the Ayung Gorge.

06 | On waking, the first views are of the rainforest.
Bedroom in the "Clear Water" master suite.

the chedi ubud | bali . indonesia

DESIGN: Kerry Hill Architects

If you were to rank the 100 most beautiful hotel swimming pools in the world, then the Chedi Ubud would be right up there at the top. Moving from the pool bar into the water, the water's surface seems to flow endlessly through the jungle and reach up to the sky. The trick here is quite simple: The pool is built along the edge of a ravine. Straight below the pool's edgeless rim, the holy Ayung River makes a sharp bend and flows away from the anthracite-coloured pool.

At water level, one gets the impression that the river is forming a viaduct over the valley, covered on each side by forested hills.

Along with its pristine natural setting, the Chedi is also located about five miles from the artist colony of Ubud, on an exposed site between tropical forests and rice-fields. The resort was developed by Kerry Hill and is somewhat more economical than the Amanresort nearby. Its 54

rooms and six suite villas stand above the ravine on stilts like treehouses. They are designed in the style of small settlements, within two blocks set along the ravine, each containing four housing units. While the architecture makes use of traditional Balinese design, it is transformed into a strict geometry.

Smooth plaster walls and concrete meet with straw roofs; terracotta tiles meet gravel or crushed rock; wood

meets glass and everything together sits amidst tropical plants.

A particularly engaging detail at the Chedi Ubud is the framework of natural pictures. Behind the beds in each room are cabinet-like wooden walls with two "furniture doors" cut in between two narrow glass windows. When opened, they present a unique view of a different piece of nature in each room.

01 | From the water's surface, the pool seems to
merge into the dense trees in the background.

02

02 | With 54 rooms and suites, the jungle
complex close to Ubud counts among
the region's larger resorts.

03 | Bedroom in one of the suites. The
wooden terrace behind the glass folding
door lies directly over the Ayung Gorge.

04 | Reception and lobby. Behind here is the
library.

05 | Open living is a basic principle in
Balinese architecture. The open-air baths
in the suites play a part in this ideal.

03
04

05

four seasons resort bali at sayan | bali . indonesia

DESIGN: John Heah

One should be careful in the use of superlatives, but it's hard to think of another way to describe the innovative architecture found at the Four Seasons Sayan where tropical forests, rice-fields and a holy river seamlessly and effortlessly blend into one.

This property is the most impressive new hotel in recent memory. There is nothing comparable to what the

Malaysian-born and London-based architect John Heah and his team of eight have created in the hills of Bali. Even the elliptical main building is unique; it's viewed initially by arriving guests as a lily pond. To reach the reception area, you must first cross a ravine via a wooden bridge held up by steel girders. All of this, however, remains invisible at first. It's only after you walk across the suspension bridge,

go down to the pond and into the spaceship-like hotel that these surroundings become apparent. Three distinct levels house the lounge, the restaurant, three separate conference rooms and a spa and fitness centre. Each level is protected against rain and sun by a broad roof, yet guests inside are still given the feeling of being seated entirely outdoors. Inside the lobby a circulating water channel acts

like an orchestra pit to separate the public from a lush stage of nature. The chattering of tropical birds accompanies meditative, ancient music, contributing to a thoroughly enchanting mood.

A total of 18 suites may be found in the side wings of the main building. They are connected along inner and outer staircases, wooden bridges and rock corridors, all

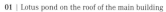

01 | Lotus pond on the roof of the main building

02 | One floor below the roof pond is the reception with lobby and bar.
Under that is the restaurant, and one floor further still are the
spa and fitness facilities.

accented by elegant canals and waterfalls. Still, it is the 28 villas that are hardest to surpass in terms of luxury and location. Moving from the slope, these villas are entered from their flat roofs and down a staircase into the outdoor living room, through the sleeping quarters with four-poster beds and into the gigantic bath with outdoor shower. A separate, wood-plank terrace surrounds a private swimming pool for each suite.

03 | From the eliptical main building, walkways and corridors lead to the 18 suites. Most are two-storey.

04 | Many of the 28 villas lie within seeing and hearing distance of the Ayung River. All have their own plunge pools.

05 | Water pool before the spa and fitness area.

01

06 | Plan of the three floors in the main building.

07 | In the villas, the open lounge extends directly to the wooden terrace, with the pool above.

08 | Internal wooden steps supported on steel tubes. External steps are made from stone and run along both sides of the building.

09 | Water is an integral component of the architecture. Here it borders the lobby and bar on the open edge of the building.

02

the legian | bali . indonesia

DESIGN: Jaya Ibrahim

Majestic waves, stretched-out beaches, white sands – all the ideal prerequisites for the construction of a resort. These conditions were exploited significantly on a dreamy beach on Bali's southwest coast where one hotel after another runs for miles along the sea shore.

This is where a full 90 percent of Bali's total tourist activity takes place. But further north, beyond the region of Seminyak, lies the Legian – set within a privileged location away from the bustle down south. But the area may not remain so hidden for long: plans call for the construction of new buildings in this still, mostly untouched area.

The Legian was originally planned as a holiday apartment development. Now, as a five-star hotel, this original design still works. Boasting 67 suites in the main building, and 10 more in the newly opened Legian Club, the Legian rises to the maximum height allowed by local authorities – one palm tree. Fourteen suites come in the two-bedroom variety reaching 150 m² in size, and featuring a terrace, as well as views of the pool, beach and the startlingly powerful Indian Ocean waves. This timeless elegance owes its origins to interior architect Jaya Ibrahim, who is originally from Jakarta and lived for several

years in London, working as a partner of Anoushka Hempel. For the colour selection, Ibrahim was inspired by the ocean. The Legian's fabrics were woven by native artisans in aquamarine. The terrazzo tiles in the bath are sand coloured and the Balinese parquet floors are made of mahogany. Separately designed, but equally luxurious is the hotel furniture, which is reminiscent of the furnishings of an old luxury steamer.

In comparison to the rooms' size, the location and the accompanying facilities, including the spa, opened in 2002 in the Legian Club, the hotel's prices have remained moderate.

01 | The hotel pool lies directly on the long,
empty beach beach, north of Seminyak and
Kuta.

02 | The hotel was originally planned as an
apartment block. Today's visitors gain from
the spacious layout of the guest quarters.

03 | Harmony between nature, furnishing and architecture.

04 | Internal room in the Legian Club villa, opened in 2002, which now houses an extensive spa facility.

05 | Each of the 67 suites has its own furnished terrace.

04 05

01 | From the pavillions built in the hills, there is a grandiose view across the trees to the sea.

banyan tree bintan | bintan . indonesia

DESIGN: Ho Kwon Cjan

In addition to their two successful resorts on Phuket and in the Maldives, Banyan Tree Hotels & Resorts have now opened their third wellness resort on the island of Bintan, which lies close to Singapore, just 45 minutes away by high-speed boat. Nature's richness unfolds in all its glory on the island and, in the north, a hillside of almost untouched vegetation rises above the beach. Coconut palms, ancient forests and mangroves provide the scenery; the actors are parrots and monkeys.

Scattered over the hillside are 72 individual villas, each different in character and each with different special features depending on its location. Some villas are built onto large rocks at the water's edge, others are in the forest or on the hilltop. The most unusual villas in visual terms must be the ones in the lush tropical forest on the hillside. These have been built on stilts, so as not to damage the tree population. Not only do they look like tree houses from the outside; inside too it is easy to feel a bit like Tarzan and Jane – in a much more luxurious setting, of course, and without the vines. The decor in all of the villas is reminiscent of the

Asian colonial style: very functional on the one hand, with clear lines and smooth polished surfaces. On the other, they are sumptuously furnished with cushions, covers and drapes. Dark wood predominates and, in sharp contrast, the colour white. This elegance is a constant and gentle reminder of days gone by, an element of nostalgia which never seems to lose its contemporary appeal. Works of art and individual architectural features, such as the villas' grass roofs, allude to the locality and to the traditions and lifestyle of the region.

All the villas have either their own reasonably sized private pool or a jacuzzi, as well as generous terraces. This allows guests to choose between the privacy of their own villa and the more public areas of the beach or the resort's main pool. Residents in villas at the top of the hill have a very good reason for choosing the first option. Their villas' main attraction is the magnificent vista of a peaceful bay or out over the South China Sea, depending on location. The architecture of the villas echoes Asian style, without imitating any one cultural design in particular.

02

The rooms all open out onto wooden sundecks around a private pool - it does not take long here for the main pool to become the focal point of activity.

At the end facing down into the valley, the water's surface appears to hover right over the edge with nothing visible to hold it back, so that looking down calls for a dash of courage. Water is the central theme throughout the resort, which is only natural, given the vast expanses of it surrounding the island. The planners have been skilful in picking up this theme and in introducing it in all kinds of variations.

Three restaurants offer plenty of culinary variety and a choice between seafood, Asian and Mediterranean specialities. And if you don't fancy walking the few steps to a restaurant in the evening, you can even dine in your own villa.

02 | A central point in the spacious villas is the swimming pool, or a jacuzzi in the less expensive versions.

03 | Hotel swimming pool in jungle style. This idyll is just 45 minutes from Singapore by speedboat.

04 | As hoteliers of the "old guard" the interiors of the hotel can sometimes be a little too plushly decorated.

04

malaysia

the datai | langkawi . malaysia

DESIGN: Kerry Hill Architects

In a small, idyllic bay northwest of the Malaysian island of Langkawi, tropical rainforests and white, sand beaches come together as one. The result: A haven from south Langkawi's overdeveloped madness in a location perhaps as perfect as paradise.

Gently cultivated by Kerry Hill, The Datai was developed within the local forests using little land, and with little damage to the old growth trees around. The hotel combines the grace of a tropical, traditional Asian temple with the functionality of modern times. Its forms are clear and geometric, typified by floors of stone and warm wooden elements. Hill has kept decorative flourishes to a minimum, trading flashy or colourful furnishings for elegant, artistic design details.

At the centre of The Datai lies its pool with ocean views. It's literally cut into the hotel's terrace, and below are offices, the lobby and a restaurant. Fanning out to the sides are accommodation wings housing 54 rooms and 13 suites. Connecting them all is a park-like network of paths, which themselves link with an additional 40 villas – each with their own sun terrace, sleeping area, breakfast veranda and towering, glass-encased ceiling.

Peek out from the tub: A lush tropical view awaits. Local woods from nearby forests are the dominant material used for the floors, fittings and specially designed furnishings. The airy, open design plan also provides guests with a sense of sleeping in the jungle itself, complete with mysterious, mystic sounds and sensations.

With an average temperature of 77° F, The Datai's climate is pleasantly moderate. Even

01 | An excellent example of how straight-
lined, contemporary architecture can
balance with lush natural surroundings

with rainforest levels of humidity, ample ventilation and an even ampler Andaman Sea breeze assure a high level of comfort.

Next door, an 18-hole golf course means that The Datai is a seaside oasis for golfers as well as pure sun-seekers. Even with its remote location, The Datai's cuisine is exquisitely familiar. Freshly caught fish and delicious seafood is served in the tree- house Thai restaurant or at the pool bar. Meanwhile at the main restaurant, a refined Malaysian menu is offered that is traditional in taste, complemented by Western embellishments.

02 | One of the 40 suites, encircled by
     tropical rainforest.

03 | Bathroom with a panoramic view
     across the jungle.

01 | Pavarotti is a regular guest who has helped to make the Pangkor Laut well known. The four residences on the 121 hectare island represent a evolution in luxury.

02 | Bedroom

03 | Private pool area. Wellness treatments can be ordered.

pangkor laut estates | lumut . malaysia

DESIGN: Baldip Singh Bullar, YTL Design Group

The new Pangkor Laut Estates at Marina Bay are so important to Malaysia's tourism industry that their opening in 2000 was officiated over by none other than Dr. Mahathir Mohamad, the nation's Prime Minister. Located on the northern coast of the privately owned Pangkor Laut island five kilometres from the Malaysian mainland, it's easy to see why Marina Bay is eyed with such pride by the Malaysian people. Boasting just nine residences – or estates – Marina Bay offers visitors the ultimate in luxury, serenity and exclusivity.

Marina Bay is divided into two distinct zones: Four estates are set along the beach, a vast expanse of sandy whiteness licked by azure waves. The remaining five villas are perched among the island's tropical forest and offer views to the east and west. Estates come in a range of sizes – two, three or four bedrooms – and also include expansive living quarters, large outdoor areas, leisure and dining pavilions, unique tropical gardens and private pools, both free-form and infinity-edge in design. While they differ in size, shape and location, all estates are decorated in typical south-east Asian designs, incorporating native fabrics and craftsmanship in their furnishings. In particular, the aesthetic influences of Malaysia's eastern Kelantan and Terengganu states are felt in the estates' decor, most notably in their intricate hand-crafted furniture.

With its tiny island home a scant 300 acres in size, Pangkor Laut Estates is compelled by circumstance, as well as a sense of duty, to respect the natural environment to the fullest extent possible. Virgin, prehistoric tropical forests cover the island and provide it with a sense of exotic adventure. Such trees were handled with particular care during the resort's construction, felled only when absolutely necessary to complete the final project.

Still, with land and seascapes bursting with everything from vines to forests, monkeys to lizards, eagles to otters and giant clams and turtles, there is ample evidence of nature's work throughout this secluded, private island. And for those who still demand more, the nearby island of Sembilan offers pristine diving conditions in the waters off the Pangkor Strait.

maldives

kanuhura beach & spa resort | lhaviyani atoll . maldives

DESIGN: Tecton Architects, Male

Quite rightly, practically every visitor to the Maldives imagines it to be pure heaven on earth. Kanuhura, with its five-star resort, opened in 2000 and is one of the country's most comprehensive spa complexes, not to mention easily among the most exquisite islands in the Maldive's chain of 20 Indian Ocean atolls and their 1190 reef sand piles. On offer is tranquility and unsurpassed luxury at prices refreshingly below the traditional top-tier level.

The island itself is one kilometre long and at its widest point 200 metres wide. It lies at the eastern edge of the largely untouched Lhaviyani Atoll, roughly 40 minutes by sea-plane north of Male, the Maldivian capital. Just the arrival flight is an experience in itself. The mainly barefoot and handsome pilots in charge of the "Maldivian Air Taxis" steer their aircraft across the sea and the Maldivian island world, barely 1000 metres in the air.

After an impressive lap-of-honour over Kanuhuru, they land effortlessly and lash their lines to the long pontoon and sea-plane gate. With a little luck, majestic, gliding rays greet guests as they make their way to land. Looking through the clear water to the white sandy bottom below, one meets fish that would normally only be found in an aquarium. Thanks to their unique, pristine and expansive nature, the Maldives are a dream destination for divers and snorkeling fans who marvel at their long coral reefs and complex underwater biology. But even restless bankers or other aquatic novices can enjoy a week or so of relaxation, fine tuning the art of doing nothing on Kanuhura.

Well, perhaps almost doing nothing. One leisurely, but highly recommended activity is an early morning jog. One has to start out just before sunrise to avoid the early day heat or the high tide. A run around the island takes a mere 15 minutes, with yielding, fine sand always underfoot. Such a journey is also the best way to witness the hotel's successful approach to island architecture.

You first see the sunning lounge-chairs lying in front of the property's 77 beach villas (70 villas at 55 m^2; five duplex villas at 104 m^2; and two suites, each 130 m^2) which are sleek, refined and made of

01

02

01 | Typical for the Maldives – wooden pontoons, straw
roofs and crystal clear waters

02 | Open-air bath in one of the water huts

03

03 | Kanuhura established itself as one of the Maldives' first wellness
complexes, and offers one of the country's most extensive
programmes.

04 | From the terrace of the water pavillion, one can clamber down a
ladder directly into the relatively shallow ocean.

05 | A simple shower.

sturdy wood. Set between strategically arranged palms and shrubs are spot lights and terracotta, along with mushroom-shaped lamps, which, come nighttime, create a romantic walkway along the beach. Along the way there are seashells to find, both natural dotting the sand, or as motifs, placed throughout the hotel's lighting, mosaics, open-air showers, on plant pots and as decorations on the buildings.

Although the hotel did not necessarily incorporate first-class architecture and interior design into its original planning, the property does distinguish itself from the majority of other resort projects in that it rejects the cookie-cutter aesthetic so often found worldwide.

Kanuhura also satisfies every desire for world-class cuisine. The buffet at the Thin Rah or Olive Tree restaurants is excellent and eclectic, reflecting the influence of chefs from nine different nations. Long trousers would appear appropriate; but leisure lovers can rest assured this is the most formal of attire the hotel demands. Laid back and relaxed is more the order at hand. And within this concept, the resort is the perfect place to soothe the soul and regenerate.

04

05

01 | The 48 luxury pavillions are romantic, but not kitsch.

02 | Measuring just 100 metres across, the island is a perfect
location for a guaranteed stress-free break.

03 | When mental relaxation is hard to achieve, a little physical
therapy can help.

banyan tree vabbinfaru | vabbinfaru . maldives

DESIGN: Ho Kwon Cian

The miniscule island of Vabbinfaru, no more than 100 metres long by 100 metres wide, lies in the lower third of the North Malé Atoll. After the strain of an overnight flight, a speedboat is the best choice of transfer for those who can scarcely wait to let the dazzling white sand trickle through their fingers. It takes only 20 minutes to reach Vabbinfaru from the airport and this is definitely the most comfortable way of crossing the shallow, crystal-clear water.

As you leave the landing stage which stretches out over the gently shelving beach, a paradise of barely imaginable exquisiteness opens up before you. Though the lively North Malé Atoll has the majority of the island hotels, and therefore more boat traffic than other atolls, the Banyan Tree Hotel & Resort stands in an exclusive, isolated position. Together with a handful of other resorts, it is

among the very best of what the Maldives have to offer at present in the way of luxury, beauty and taste.

Rather than an enormous club resort dominating the island, the 48 guest villas are nicely spread out in the welcome shade of the dense coconut palms. Romantic island seclusion is guaranteed. Any stressed city-dwellers who come here to spend an intimate fortnight with their loved one ought not to suffer from claustrophobia, however. In spite of the wide range of activities on offer, there are always some people who cannot sit still for five minutes. By the third day, they are leaping backwards and forwards around the island, only to keep ending up at the water's edge. Such visitors would be well advised to pack very few clothes but to bring with them instead a good supply of books they have always been meaning to read.

However, the tastefully and luxuriously appointed round villas with their characteristic pointed straw roofs and wooden verandahs are inviting places that deserve better than to be used merely as an expensive place to sleep. So immerse yourself in a good novel in the shade of a palm tree and look up from time to time to check if the sea is still where it was – the sort of exercise that promises true relaxation and will renew the energy in your physical and spiritual batteries. The small houses offer every conceivable luxury, but the planners have also managed to create a refreshingly provisional impression. The generous, sumptuous beds with their delicate mosquito nets stand in the centre of the room, surrounded by high doors. The curtains at the windows billow out in a light breeze, gently fanning fresh air into the room.

The Banyan Tree Spa is a professional complement to the natural well-being guests feel on the island. The spa is based on a holistic approach to health which aims to create a balance between mind and body, employing massages and treatments rooted in ancient Asian tradition. The intimate spa pavilions, where optical and acoustic factors help to enhance the physical treatments, are an important element in the sensual experience. The spa pavilions combine aesthetically pleasing architecture – the result of a local building style in harmony with nature – and the exotic romance of the natural surroundings, including the sound of the sea.

four seasons resort kuda huraa | kuda huraa . maldives

DESIGN: Grounds Kent Architects, Anke Zieck

A tiny island edged with dazzling white sand in the middle of crystal-clear, turquoise blue shimmering water, and this entire paradise reserved for gentle wellness pleasures – the notion of the spa is entering a new dimension. The name of the island next to the Four Seasons Resort island of Kuda Huraa is Hura Fundhu, which means 'island of many coconut palms'. It lies in the North Malé

Atoll, 25 minutes by high-speed boat from the capital Malé.

Even the transfer from the resort island by 'dhoni' – a traditional wooden boat used by the locals – puts guests in the mood for the spa experience. Your therapist awaits at the 20-metre-long wooden landing stage. The spa's reception area resembles a Moroccan Bedouin tent, and

you are served delicious ginger lemon tea as you relax on soft cream-coloured pillows. All five massage pavillions are built out over the sea on stilts. Large glass sliding doors can be opened if required, letting in a cooling sea breeze, and large picture windows have been installed underneath the massage couches so that, during a meditative, gentle Balinese massage, guests can watch the fish and other sea

creatures moving in and out of the coral. Hardly any guests opt to have meditation or atmospheric sounds piped in as a background, a feature of spas elsewhere, preferring to abandon themselves to the mesmerising, soothing sound of the Indian Ocean.

The five pavillions can also be used by couples; each one has a dressing area where there is an open inner courtyard with

01 | The 106 reed thatched guest pavillions are distributed across the five hectare island, Kuda Huraa.

02

02 | The resort's spa complex lies on the neighbouring island of Hura Fundhu.

03 | All five massage pavillions are built on stilts over the sea.

04 | The simplicity of the guestrooms certainly adds to the feeling of well-being.

05 | F

03

04

05

greenery, outdoor showers and a tub with frangipani flowers. Step-down pools full of hibiscus flowers and roses offer plenty of space for two to cool off together after the rigours of a steam bath.

In this totally private and secluded setting, guests can enjoy an Oceanic Ritual, an Ayurvedic Shiro Dhara, a Maldivian Monsoon Ritual, or can have a Facial Lepa to detox and nourish the facial skin. The treatments offered come from Thailand, Bali and India, but have been enriched by Maldivian traditions.

The luxury resort's 106 guest pavillions, built of wood in the traditional style and with thatch roofs, are spread over Kuda Huraa island's five hectares. Most spectacular are the water bungalows built on stilts just above the shallow ocean; they are unusually generous in size, and you cannot help feeling that you are floating on air above the magnificent coral with its millions of exotic fish.

01 | The seemingly endless ocean around
Soneva Gili acts as a barrier to stress
and hectic of any kind.

soneva gili | lankanfushi . maldives

DESIGN: Sonu + Eva Shivdasani

The Soneva Gili Resort is not actually on dry land at all – in so far as that description can be applied to the mini piles of sand that are the Maldives. Instead, the 37 individual wooden villas are arranged around Lankanfushi island in the Lankanfushi lagoon. Unlike its sister hotel Soneva Fushi, also a member of Eva Malmström and Sonu Shivdasani's Six Senses Group, Soneva Gili – opened in 2002 – is one of the first resorts anywhere to have accommodation built entirely above water – water that is indescribably clear. Most of the villas have bridges linking them

to the "land", although the only way for guests to reach eight "Crusoe residences" is by private rowing boat. Only the resort's public areas are on the island itself: the reception, restaurant, pool and sports facilities.

The choice of accommodation ranges from a "standard" suite to a residence on two levels with its own private kitchen and several bedrooms. A feature shared by all the villas is their architectural style. Suggestive of a temporary structure, they bring to mind childlike fantasies of building a tree house or a hideaway in

the woods. The buildings appear to have been built little by little, as though people had kept on adding another living space onto their existing structure – a living room, a second bedroom, a sun terrace. It seems as though other sections could be added as and when, should the need arise. This rather unfinished impression is precisely what gives the resort its special charm; you cannot feel you are living Robinson Crusoe-style in a house that was planned and built to perfect specifications.

The villas, which are built entirely of wood, stand on stilts

just above the surface of the water. Some walls are left open, allowing plenty of air to circulate, making for cool indoor temperatures, which are desirable in the local climate. The roof trusses in the individual rooms have been left visible. Mosquito nets billow in the wafting breeze. It all creates an airy impression, the perfect retreat for when it gets too hot outside in the sun. Beds have crisp white sheets and are ideal for an afternoon nap, or maybe in the walled recess, furnished with a day bed complete with colourful bolsters and cushions. Afternoons can be shared

02 | The resort, opened in 2002, offers a blend of
adventure, dreams and luxury.

03 | The conglomerate of huts includes 15 multi-
suite residences and 29 villa suites, often
with roof terrace, with divan and jacuzzi.

04 | Despite the salty air, the architects have
incorporated full-room glazing into their
design.

05 | Almost as if on a luxury ship, but without the
swaying.

between the turquoise water of the lagoon and the terrace that floats on the water beside the villa, before you cross the bridge to the island for dinner later on. The al fresco restaurant serves light regional specialities to be enjoyed whilst watching the sunset from the terrace. For a romantic interlude, however, there can be nothing better than your own roof terrace, which in some villas has a couch-style mattress, where guests can spend the night

beneath an indigo, starlit sky. An even more tempting alternative is the jacuzzi built into the wooden floor.

As for sport, everything revolves around the water: swimming, surfing, sailing, deep-sea fishing, snorkelling and – the main attraction – diving. But sportsmen who prefer activities on dry land do not have to go without their tennis, jogging or their regular fitness programme. The range of treatments and facilities

offered at the spa also deserves a special mention. Like the guest rooms, most of the treatment rooms and the fitness area are suspended above the water in a collection of villas with extensive wooden sun decks.

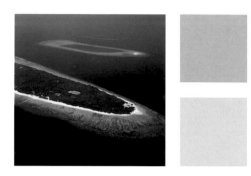

soneva fushi | kunfunadhoo . maldives

DESIGN : Dick Wells, Tebbott & Wells, Ismael Rasheed, Riyan Design Diek

The resort on the private island of Kunfundahoo, a 45 minute flight from Male, is a rarity in the world of luxury hotels, whose exceptional qualities lie in the personal style of its design. The island, a 1.5km long and 400m wide sliver in the sea, is edged with white sand beaches and, of course, iconic coconut palms. Naturally, its emerald-green waters are crystal clear; so clear in fact, you can see tiny, coloured fish and coral without ever wetting your feet.

With more than 250 types of plant life, including such tasty examples as mango and papaya, this mini-jungle on the sand north of the Baa Atoll, is an Eden. Even the wildlife here is impressive, and is some of the most lively in the entire Maldivian island chain. And for those adventurous enough to venture through this tropical maze, your reward will be a veritable zoo full of wild rabbits, chickens, lizards and – come dusk – exotic flying foxes.

The hotel complex itself is unquestionably unique and aesthetically authentic. Its owners, Swedish ex-model Eva Malmström and Indian businessman Sono Shivdasana, form a powerful and innovative pair, who've transformed their uncompromising concept of a luxury retreat into a hallmark for their ever-developing hotel business. The results are 62 spacious villas and 25 double rooms tucked away in six separate jungle compounds

created by architects to offer the littlest possible opportunity for paparazzi and preying eyes to snap visiting celeb-guests.

Of course all villas and rooms boast direct access to the water along with picture-perfect, see-it-to-believe-it sea vistas. Here, the scale of luxury can literally go through the roof, depending on the level of accommodation. There are the indulgent Rehendi rooms, or the two-floor, 60 m^2 Crusoe villas. Or bigger still, the 80 m^2

01 | Sixty-two spacious beach villas and 25 double
rooms are scattered aross the 1.5 kilometre long
and 400 metre wide island.

Soneva Fushi villa and their
suite counterparts sized at 96
m². Still not satisfied? Then
upgrade to the resort's best
bet, the 190 m² presidential
villa. Such style does not come
cheap and guests willing to
shell out US$3,500 per night
during the winter high season
are also invited to bring their
personal butler or nanny. And
why not? A separate en-suite
room can be arranged
especially for them.

Each of the palm-thatched

02

03

premium suites has its own private garden filled with lush vegetation, which shields the rooms from even the closest neighbours. Building materials, mainly woods and white-painted stone, are all organic and were sourced from local forests and quarries whenever possible. Stairway and balcony railings were crafted from the branches of small tree trunks, while all chairs, seating, tables and beds were cut from rough wood. This "Flintstones"-styled design lends these noble

beach-side chalets a cosy, Robinson Crusoe romance without resorting to kitsch.

The rooms' dominant ecological motifs are nicely contrasted by white and beige soft furnishings and linens, rough-cut stone floors, large windows and well-placed lighting. And while all rooms were finished to the highest standards, specific furnishings and architecture vary according to villa type. In the Rehendi rooms, for instance,

beds are placed just above the floor and are more toned-down in scale. At the opposite extreme, the Crusoe and Soneva Fushi villas are larger and more opulent in decor.

Still, nothing is really missing at the Soneva Fushi, where the guest villas are merely one aspect of an entire holiday experience. The owners and management place particular emphasis on exceptional food and an on-site, integrated wellness centre. Here, eight

treatment rooms are available for massage and other body treatments. In the restaurant, Me Dhunyie, the chef serves excellent menus based on an "East meets West" theme, unusual to the Maldives. With so many luxury amenities, Soneva Fushi is among the most prestigious resorts across these islands.

02 | The mixture of archaic forms and light colours is typical of the interior design.

03 | Glazed living room / bathroom with seaview.

04 | Bedroom in one of the "simpler" Rehendi villas.

05 | Bedroom in the Soneva Fushi suite.

04 05

taiwan

the lalu | sun moon lake . taiwan

DESIGN: Kerry Hill

"Our concept is to create hotels with a special style in special places. A mixture that brings together the natural environment and international luxury standards. Each personal note, each little extra that separates us from the rest, lifts us from the ordinary." A claim to exclusivity for The Lalu, from its General Manager, Larry van Ooyen.

The Lalu lies in the middle of Taiwan. From the landscape of its location alone, the hotel offers an impressive panorama. In the mountainous central region of the Chinese island state, the property is directly on the shores of Sun Moon Lake. A lake that the local Shao people regard as having mystical powers. These inhabitants also gave the body of water its unusual name, taken from its shape. The banks on one side curve into a sickle form, and towards the mountains they bow outwards like the sun. It is not just in the evenings that the water projects a calming influence. The whole landscape could have been made for meditative moments. Perhaps it was for this very reason that Chiang Kai Shek, the political leader of the Chinese nationalists, had his summer-house here. Now architect Kerry Hill has recreated another centre of peace in The Lalu. A building complex comprised of suites and private villas with their own gardens, swimming pool and fireplaces. Alongside is the hotel's own spa, four gastronomy outlets, including a traditional Chinese teahouse and a Japanese restaurant. In the design and choice of furniture, the rooms are defined by a strict adherence to form, and a distinguishing east-Asian modernism. The spaces almost seem like still-lifes, but radiate comfort and compactness, fitting the surrounding environs. In a generous manner, The Lalu offers a place for regeneration and re-concentration of body and soul. Numerous paths lead to old temples, pagodas and tea plantations in the immediate area. Angling in the lake's waters is an alternative exercise in silence and patience, and its depths are home to a delicious reward – the so-called president fish.

01 | Since 2002, The Lalu's guests, resting above the Sun Moon Lake, have been able to enjoy the same views that once delighted Chiang Kai Shek.

02 03

04

05

02 | The elegant harmony of form and colour.

03 | A light touch of the 1950's in the design of the hotel's
rooms and suites.

04 | Bathroom with sliding glass door and open-air shower.

05 | Fire room.

thailand

the sukhothai | bangkok . thailand

DESIGN: Edward Tuttle

Few hotels live up to their names like the Sukhothai. In Thai, the word translates into "Dawn of Happiness" and is also the name of Thailand's first kingdom, which was established in 1238. But then again Bangkok's Sukhothai Hotel is unlike any hotel in this bustling metropolis.

Opened in 1991 and designed by Edward Tuttle, whose Amanpuri on the island of Phuket is one of Thailand's most idyllic retreats, the Sukhothai pairs a pure minimalist aesthetic with the best of architectural traditions, craftsmanship and local materials. Set upon a six-acre site right in the heart of Bangkok, the Sukhothai is defined both by its impressive buildings and its equally impressive gardens and water ponds. The latter are the first things visitors spy when entering the property: Lily-filled ponds and reflecting pools with traditional, gold-leaf religious monuments, known as chedis, which ring nearly every part of the hotel complex.

The Sukhothai's 146 rooms and 78 suites are housed in a series of four- to nine-story edifices which surround open courtyards and are linked by logically flowing colonnades and hallways. Rather than face the outside and its perhaps uninspiring Bangkok view, rooms instead face inward and look onto the hotel's stunning water gardens. Another novel twist is the Sukhothai's corridors – open-air passageways shielded from the outside by heavy wooden panels. The structures have been created to evoke the palaces of ancient Siam, only with a more restrained tone using clean, straight lines rather than sinuous curves, and subtle detailing in place of more bombastic artwork and statues.

The rooms themselves come in a slew of sizes and layouts, with some offering refreshing terraces and others located alongside ground floor gardens. All rooms contain bathrooms of truly unique accents, crafted mainly from teak and massive in size. The rooms are decorated with silk panels coloured in rust, gold and green, along with carpets woven from native fabrics and additional teak furnishings.

Because of the stifling heat, the Sukhothai has perhaps become equally known for its elegant 25m swimming pool as its, oversized rooms. The

02 | The pagoda-form, Buddhist chedis are are central to the overall design concept.

03 | Reception hall.

04 | The middle category superior rooms offer more space than some suites in other hotels.

05 | Reception, where both staff and decoration are unassuming.

03

04

05

rectangular pool is bordered by leisurely lounge chairs with parasols and is enveloped in the verdant greenery of the hotel's gardens. Equally renowned is "Celadon", the hotel's Thai restaurant. Set within an almost free-flowing pavillion on a stunning lily pond, "Celadon" is where Bangkok's elite dine on their national cuisine along with a who's who of local expatriates and visiting celebrities. In a city known for its luxury hotels and

their legendary service, extras such as "Celadon" help the Sukhothai stand out from the crowd.

01 | Since its opening in 1999, the Lanna
Spa has been constantly among the
world's top ten.

regent chiang mai resort & spa| chiang mai . thailand
DESIGN: Chulathat Kitibutr, Abacus Design, Bensely Design

The Regent Chiang Mai is situated in northern Thailand in Mae Rim Valley, about half an hour's drive from the centre of Chiang Mai and from the airport. Belonging to the Four Seasons Group, the Regent Chiang Mai is its sole luxury resort and since opening has managed to retain its position at the zenith of the hotel trade. It is regularly listed in the top 10 world-class hotels selected annually by Condé Nast Traveller magazine.

Although the resort itself is resplendent in its successful design, promising pure relaxation, its location is also a good starting point for excursions to the surrounding area. One tourist option is a trip to the Chiang Mai night market, offering bustling activity as well as hand-crafted bargains. Watch elephants at work in the nearby elephant farm and applaud as they perform tricks with their owners. Nature lovers will encounter dense jungle and national parks. Slightly further afield, the hotel offers expeditions to the Thai Alps, Mae Hong Son, to the Golden Triangle (Laos, Myanmar, Thailand) or to Mandalay. The whole region shines with its thousands of Buddhist temples.

Back at Regent Chiang Mai, the resort's beauty and wellness centre deservedly enjoys a world-wide reputation. The Lanna Spa, opened in 1999, is impressive on account of its location surrounded by colourful tropical splendour, over 40 gardeners ensure that it is kept beautiful. Its architecture is also an attraction: traditional, but given a sensitive modern touch. Typical of Lanna architecture, which dominates this region and northern Thailand, is the filigree wooden style of building with numerous small terraces, bridges, oriels and towers as well as steep, pointed roofs. Lanna roughly translates as "Land of a million rice fields" and describes the kingdom which enjoyed its peak around 700 years ago when it was still part of Burma. Its influences can be seen today in architecture, art and handcrafts. It is an interpretation of the concept of accurate division and terracing and, moreover, a demonstration of careful treatment of nature. The three-storied spa villa is exemplary of the building style and its interior design is a contemporary representation.

Warm wood is set against cool stone, filigree carvings against plain, smooth surfaces, and heavy linen fabrics against light silk scarves. These combinations have been perfectly weighed in terms of materials and colours. The almost labyrinthine architecture, full of nooks and crannies, provides a fitting frame within which details can constantly be discovered, rather like piecing together a puzzle. Altogether, the complex houses seven generous treatment suites with a bathing area and massage and relaxation zones. The three suites on the ground floor also have a garden, and the penthouse has a roof terrace with open-air bath tub. The closed units are designed to give guests a feeling of utmost privacy. For this reason it is popular with famous guests who are, like everyone else here, protected by "Naga", a huge snake sculpture coiled around the building, encouraging any evil spirits to immediately take their leave.

But it is not only the spa and the similarly structured private residences that offer shining examples of stimulating design. The whole resort has the air of a kingdom steeped in legend, especially during sunrise or sunset when the property is illuminated by wind lights, papyrus lanterns and torches. The resort is arranged in the form of a horse shoe around an extended rice field. The reception, restaurants, boutique, library and pool area, with a wooden terrace jutting out directly over the fields, have been built on a slight slope on the "closed side". Above, as well as to the right and left of the rice-fields are 64 pavilions and 16 residential suites on stilts, the latter covering over 300 m². While some of the residential suites have their own private plunge pool, all the pavillion suites are

02 | The 64 pavillions and 16 Residence suites are all raised on stilts, collected in a horseshoe form around rice-fields.

03 | View over the swimming pool to the outlines of the Doi Suthep Doi Pui mountains.

divided into an enclosed sleeping/living area and an almost equally large roofed terrace. From here, guests can savour the fascinating view across the gentle hilly landscape and, on a clear day, see the outline of the Doi Suthep Doi Pui mountains.

The Sala Mae Rim cuisine is excellent. Alongside outstanding Thai meals it also serves selected dishes from the north of the country. Among the specialities are Chiang Mai curry noodle soup and chicken salad served on a banana leaf with plenty of chilli. Those who fall in love with these delicious morsels can recreate them at the hotel's popular cookery course.

04

05 06

04 | Statues, Buddhist symbols and fine arranged plants are dotted around the complex.

05 | A revitalising shower.

06 | From the suites in the upper floors, wooden bridges lead to private, furnished terrace.

07 | Unity and balance are central themes at the spa.

08 | The high ceilings in the bedrooms allow for good circulation of air.

07 08

chiva som | hua hin . thailand

DESIGN: Jean Paul Blissett, Syntax Group

On the beach, a small group are playing boules. Just a few, all sharing a satisfied, relaxed chuckle. Not far away, a little further along the sand, a more meditative cluster is practising Tai Chi. Focussed and peaceful, they slowly, deliberately move, just metres from the foaming surf. A shallow breeze flicks across the water, and the bay is almost silent. A place of quietness on the Gulf of Siam.

This is the "Haven of Life". What sounds like the title of a poem is the sonorous translation of Chiva Som; an international health resort, with its own special philosophy. Refuelling is the order of the day, holistic and complete. Here, body, soul and spirit can be brought into dry-dock for a recharge and overhaul. The

target is to regenerate and lay the foundations for a healthy and quality-conscious life ahead. The resort promotes a deep-rooted lifestyle, influenced by Buddhist meditation and long traditions of contemplation.

The Chiva Som is an exclusive environment for this experience of fulfillment. As part of an area belonging to the royal palace at Hua Hin, the resort is embedded in exotic gardens, and close to a beach reserved for only a select few. A natural, nearly untouched panorama serves as scenery for an almost inexhaustible range of recreational activities and treatments: From anti-aging to spa and hydrotherapies, from numerous wellness and beauty programmes, to dance and fitness training. Medical doctors

and therapists consult with each guest and arrange their programmes on an individual basis. Four employees take care of each visitor, and that with the typical warm-heartedness of the Thai people.

Concentration on the fundamental is the message that penetrates the architecture and design of the complex. The houses and pavillions, with their pointed, gabled roofs, appear as temples or pagodas. Public rooms share a similarity to the local teahouses, with free views across the ocean, furnished with natural fabrics. More than anywhere else, the spring baths and treatment rooms combine simple forms with noble materials – sleek elegance, with a love for detail.

The same continues in the resort's cuisine. All ingredients are sourced from the hotel's own ecological gardens. The healthy, delicious menus served are a cause for meditation in themselves, and not just their decoration. Their layers of flavour are surely the culinary equivalent to an ever-expanding mantra.

01 | Chiva Som – Haven of Life – is one of the few resorts in the world devoted to holistic medicine.

02 | The complex is shaped by traditional Thai architecture and modern, theraputic practice.

03 | Buddhist elements are just as much a part of the healing methods used as orthodox western ideas.

01

03

01 | Formerly a club complex, today a calm, aesthetic wellness resort.
Where an amphitheatre was once the centre of entertainment is
now a meditative lotus pond.

02 | Sand, water, stone and wood. A collage of materials from the
"Kindergarten" pools.

evason hua hin | hua hin . thailand

DESIGN: Bernhard Bohnenberger, Sonu + Eva Shivadasani

Had Prince Chakrabongse, at the start of the 20th Century, not so loved the long beaches of this area, its quite possible that today Hua Hin would not even be a stop on the railway between Bangkok and Singapore. The Thai royal family chose this introspective town in the province of Prachuap Khiri Khan, on the Gulf of Siam, as their summer residence, and brought a whole entourage of holiday guests along with them. Unlike Pattaya, lying opposite, the area remained protected, however, from enormous growth and mass tourism. As the country's oldest seaside resort, a number of hotels and apartment blocks sprang up along the beaches, where Thailand's upper classes could spend their weekends and weeks off. Luckily, the expanse of seashore meant that these unpleasant structures were built far apart from one another, diluting what would otherwise have been an architectural catastrophy.

Thirty kilometres south of Hua Hin, the owners of the Bangkok based hotel company Six Senses, Eva Malmström and Sono Shivdasani, have entered into a joint venture with Deutsche Bank, and transformed the former "Club Aldiana" into the newest of the Evason resorts. The restructured property, which was once a package-holiday style family club, opened with its new identity at the beginning of 2002. Its local area promises peace and endless sandy beach, miles away from the tourist traps. The drive from Bangkok takes nearly four hours with a car or bus, and with the train, almost five. Although this journey is an adventure in itself, it is long and certainly presents a bar to some guests. There is also an airport, although this is only served from Bangkok twice a day. Those that wish to see the new hotel on the Bay of Pranburi, need to bring plenty of one particular commodity with them: time.

But patience is always rewarded. The complex still has an air of "club" about it, although with a completely altered philosophy. Where sport, kids' games and animation were once the most appealing features, the emphasis has changed to relaxation and wellness for a different class of visitor. A clear example of the change brought about by the Swedish-Indian business couple can be seen at what used to be the property's outdoor amphitheatre, which has now been reborn as a

lotus pond. From a group of old guest rooms, they have also created an extensive spa specializing in complete therapies. The balance that the planners have achieved is impressive, taking in external and internal architecture, interior design, using water and vegetation as tools. The treatment rooms, for example, are partially housed in huts without walls, where the floor is lower than the surrounding ponds. As one is massaged, the body lies at the same level

as the water, increasing the meditative effect.

The dominant material used in the flooring is a mixture made of sandstone. The colour and texture blends perfectly with the tropical climate. Lush plants are used as decoration and contrast to this calm surface, as are dark brown wood tones, earth-coloured upholstery and archaic furnishings. Over an area of 20 hectares, 185 guestrooms in differing catagories are

distributed. From the Evason rooms and studios, the quarters become larger, with deluxe studios measuring 60 m², and the 40 large villas covering 110 m², complete with private pool and open-air bath. The same fresh design is common to all rooms, regardless of size, with comfortable beds, beautiful bathrooms and a wealth of decorative details.

Guests can choose from three restaurants. All are good, but

particularly worth trying is "The Other Restaurant", that sits over the newly laid lotus pond. Its Australian chef prepares fine fusion cuisine. "The Restaurant" serves breakfast and theme buffets that change daily, while wood-oven pizzas and pasta is offered at the beach restaurant. The General Manager is particularly proud of his wine cellar, where over 240 different types are available. The most popular late afternoon hangout is the

03 | In the background, the entrance to the wellness centre's treatment rooms.

04 | Washbasin in the WC behind the restaurant.

05 | One of the most beautiful pool villas, almost on the beach. Two sliding, wooden partitions allow for privacy or an open view of the sea.

05

two storey bar, just a few metres from the beach. On huge, colourful couches on the top floor – a covered verandah – the right mix of music, moonlight and a warm breeze can make for a romantic evening.

06 07

06 | Library with internet terminals and billiard table.

07 | The property's 20 hectares has 185 guestrooms, ranging
in size from simple 40 m² rooms to 110 m² villas...

08 | ...with their own pools and open-air baths.

muang kulaypan | koh samui . thailand

DESIGN: M.L. Archava Varavana

Light, cooling breezes rush through the palms which line this stretch of Koh Samui's Chaweng Beach. Flat, damp sand gently gives way underfoot while moist air intensifies the scent of saltwater and local greenery. It's a perfect location for the pursuit of serenity and contentment, two of the dominant elements at the Muang Kulaypan Hotel.

Opened in December 1996 by architect M. L. Archava Varvana and owner Khun Udomdej Bunyaraksh, the hotels combines Zen Buddhist philosophies with local customs and traditions. From the beginning of the property's simple two-storey construction, these beliefs were put into practice as the area's natural contours and vegetation were sensitively preserved to respect the hotel's environment.

A strong spiritual thread is also found in the hotel's interiors. Clean, natural materials and colours are blended with minimalist refinement. There are greys, browns and beiges to help maintain the resort's subdued atmosphere, along with beds on raised wooden stages allowing guests to sleep close to the earth, while mirrors are used to chase away evil spirits in accordance with Buddhist temple traditions.

The Javanese style of low-slung roofs is also an integral part of the the hotel's aesthetic and spiritual concept. Adorned with sculptures of seven young children, the roof's design demands that guests bow their heads on entry, which signifies humility and respect in local culture. Four of these children hold sacred objects: two with golden flowers, a drum and a triangular flag for the remaining pair – objects adopted by the ancient Thai royal courts as symbols of luck and protection for those around them. The remaining three children are symbolic as well, offering the traditional Thai salute, or wai, to greet guests.

Adding a mysterious note to the entire property is the hotel's black-tiled pool, a place of contemplation and relaxation. Its unusual colour and simple style reflect the Muang Kulaypan's overall concept: a place of hip, essential luxuriousness which offers guests enough space to revel in their own peace of mind while still discovering all the hotel has to offer.

01 | The long, two-storey structures face the
     sea, wrapped around a mysterious
     black-tiled pool.

02 | The arcaded walkways are accented with
     art objects.

03 | East-West style is prevalent in the
     design of the 41 guestrooms.

amanpuri | phuket . thailand

DESIGN: Edward Tuttle

In the still young Renaissance of well designed hotels, this resort, conceived by the visionary entrepreneur and globetrotter Adrian Zecha, is well among the example-giving ancestors. When he built it together with his architectural partner Edward Tuttle in 1988 near the exceptionally beautiful Pansea Bay, it was a sensation. It was one of the first resorts which took up the idea of a small village, with its rooms spread out into individual, luxurious buildings on stakes, instead of combining them all into a single building.

Forty generously proportioned guest pavillions are built around the bay into the palm tree forest, and interconnected by a maze-like system of stairs and paths. In addition to this there are privately owned mansions with two to four beds and separate swimming pools. The choice of materials and the details of the design closely follow traditional Thai architecture, yet the style is plainer and less ornamental. In the interiors, reddish and brown tropical woods from the area dominate. Together with local granite in the baths and pastel coloured textiles they create a serene environment.

From an architectural point of view the rooms are minimalistic in their geometry, even strictly classical. They are, however, everything but cold. Even the warm colours of the building materials themselves create an inviting impression of comfort. Appropriate for the climate, they all are equipped with a large terrace, which joins with the interior via sliding panels. Edward Tuttle was inspired in his planning by the architecture of Buddhist temples. He reduced the luxuriant variety of decorative elements he found there to a minimum and created a highly attractive contemporary interpretation.

After almost 15 years of operation and straining climatic conditions the complex has lost none of its attraction. "We consistently take good care of it", says director Ferdinand Wortelboer, "but we haven't made the slightest change to the initial design." Those who come to visit Amanpuri and don't know the resort's age would not be able to guess it. It appears as if it had only opened recently. The design is still up-to-date and has successfully avoided any short-term fashions. With its example-giving character, one might call the property a "modern classic" even today.

01 | When Adrian Zecha and Edward
Tuttle completed the Amanpuri in
1988, it was an out and out
sensation. It still remains an
example for newer resorts.

02 | Even after 15 years, the elegant,
slick rooms look fresh and now.
Sliding doors separate the
internal space from the terrace.

03

03 | Since 2002, the resort has offered
   guests an extensive wellness facility.

04 | Wood is the dominant building material
   in the treatment rooms.

05 | Spa terrace. The architectural team have
   successfully chosen materials that
   blend with the tropical environment.

04 05

The resort's main eye-catcher is the narrow, 25 metre swimming pool. Its flat, overflowing rim creates a visually seamless connection to the Andaman Sea. Successors of this design can nowadays be found frequently, but the pool ranks among the first examples to be made completely of granite. This lends a resplendent mixture of night-blue and greenish colours to the water, which stands out against the deep blue of the ocean.

Around this centre, the bar and the two restaurants are located. One offers a combination of Thai and European cuisine, the other offers Italian dishes. The most recent highlight is the spa, which was opened at the end of 2001. With its vitreous walls and expansive, wooden terraces, it is located on a hill behind the main buildings. From here the guests can enjoy a wonderful view of the neighbouring bay and Laguna Phuket. Nature, architecture and spa treatments are harmoniously united here and promise a meditative, inspiring experience.

banyan tree phuket | phuket . thailand

DESIGN: Ho Kwon Cjan

Twenty years ago, this region was a barren swamp. With the variety of wonderful bays and fine sandy beaches that Phuket has to offer, it is astounding that this area, 15 kilometres south of the airport, should have developed into a tourist attraction. The mixture of flat land, natural lagoon and a five-kilometre-long beach was obviously appealling to the investors. So much so, that they drained the swamp, landscaped the lagoon and, alongside five more-or-less luxury hotels, created an integrated holiday park with restaurants and boutiques. The different resorts of the "Laguna Phuket" can be reached by a free service bus and cosy little excursion boats, that chug along the canals and waterways. Was it not for the natural surroundings, with mountains, tropical plants and the sea, one might imagine oneself to be in a plastic, Asian form of Disneyland. Everything is a little bit cute, very orderly and marked by an outstanding infrastructure.

Visitors looking for wild, untouched nature here will be dissappointed, but a huge choice of day-trips into spectacular and well-known natural scenery slightly further away is offered. To the Bay of Phang Nga, for example, with its strange limestone cliffs, or to the James Bond island of Ko Tapu, backdrop for the film "The Man With The Golden Gun". The two neighbouring islands, Ko Phi Phi and Krabi, also have a magnetic attraction, providing some of the best images for the movie "The Beach", starring Leonardo diCaprio.

Perhaps it is exactly this option that makes the Laguna Phuket such a popular destination. By day, visitors can venture out into the surrounding environment and return to the comfort of a safe haven as the evening draws in. A further reason for many is the 18-hole World Cup golf course nearby, and its accompanying hotels and restaurants.

Banyan Tree Resort, however, offers the highest level of luxury. Not only does the golf course form part of the hotel's complex, the property also puts an extensive wellness and health centre at its guests' disposal. The philosophy is one of holistic treatment, and particular value is placed on the balance between architecture and nature, service and comfort. The aim

01

01 | "Sanctuary for the Senses" is the
central message of the Banyan
Tree Resort.

02 | Typically Thai are the steep roofs,
which create a comfortable
temperature inside the buildings.

02

03   04

for both Banyan Tree Hotels & Resorts, and its sister spa management company, Andara Spa, is to provide a "Sanctuary for the Senses". With its own academy for the training and further education of staff, the spa counts among the largest in Asia.

This commitment to the development of its employees' knowledge not only has positive effects in the service

the spa affords its guests, but also in the property's wider social sphere. The hotel's company constantly renews and furthers its workers' professional skills, creating a motivated and extremely able group, which in turn has a clear influence on the atmosphere and success of the spa. This vocational aspect is supplemented by bodies such as the Laguna Phuket Foundation for Education,

which regularly provides financial support to local educational projects. A childcare centre is another facility that Banyan Tree has set up, directly benefitting upto 200 children from the surrounding areas. Further social commitment is shown in elderly care projects and sponsorship of culture and art.

The architecture of the 109 guest villas also shows a

certain respect for local culture and art. Throughout the tropical complex's gardens, tended by over 40 gardeners, the region's typical steep roofs can be seen. Inside, the villas are fitted with warm wooden floors and rugs. The furnishings are elegant and dignified, although not conservative. The planners have given most thought to space and have certainly not been mean in the supply of this

03 | Living room in one of the 109 guestrooms.

04 | The external walls are frequently textured.

05 | One of the new, modernly designed suites with pool, near
the lagoon.

05

architectural commodity. The smallest Garden Villas are 170 m² large, and the biggest Pool Villas measure up to 350 m², with private swimming pools 10m long – ideal for more than just a paddle. The Top Suites, completed at the beginning of 2002, are immediately on the lagoon, and distinguish themselves through a markedly modern design. The bedrooms lie, like a terrace, over a lotus pond, with just a sheet of glass, from floor to ceiling, separating the bed from nature.

01 | The Chedi shares the Pansea Bay with the
Amanpuri.

02 | The resort has 98 one-bedroom pavillions
and 19 two-bedroom pavillions.

03 | A typical decorative touch.

the chedi phuket | phuket . thailand

DESIGN: Edward Tuttle, Jon Vorapot Sonton

When rich, green, tropical forests meet snow-white, sandy beaches running along deep blue seas, the location rarely remains quiet for long, especially when such a paradise is already somewhat developed. And so it was with the Thai island of Phuket. Located about an hour's flight from Bangkok, this regularly serviced island retreat is easy to reach from the Thai capital. Because of its proximity, Phuket has quickly developed into a popular vacation destination not just with Thais, but also with Europeans. Yet, even with the hustle and bustle that has accompanied Phuket's development over the past decade, there are still, fortunately, a host of peaceful and practically untouched oases. The coastline along Pansea Bay is one such place, and here lucky travellers can land upon the Chedi, the more reasonably priced sister resort to the legendary Amanpuri.

The Chedi's architectonic style is a mixture of traditional Thai designs and modern functionality brought together through careful planning and the execution of geometric forms with the natural, organic shapes of native palms, bushes, shrubs and rocks. Unsurprisingly, the Chedi's relationship with Amanpuri is aesthetically evident. Like that beloved resort, the Chedi's basic design suggestions originated from the American architect Edward Tuttle, who lives both in Paris and Thailand. Tuttle was later aided by Bangkok-based designer Jon Vorapot Somton, and together the pair created the perfect blend of the traditional and inspirational. The Chedi stands as luxury without swank, intimacy without isolation, affluence without opulence – the entire complex is marked by a consistent and reserved elegance.

04 | A bath with a view in one of the spa
    pavillions.

05 | Reduced design in the guestrooms - man
    of them have oustanding views of the
    ocean.

06 | 07 Slick sun-loungers and simple white
    parasols count among the property's
    details that add to the overall design
    quality.

04

The Chedi's 89 one-bedroom and 19 two-bedroom villas create a resort that is more like a village. Linked with three restaurants, a bar, library, boutique, conference centre, tennis courts, swimming pool and a world-class wellness centre and spa, one would not be surprised to find the Chedi a hub of activity and excitement. But thanks to their concealed position between trees and bushes, the villas themselves provide a strong sense of peacefulness, aided by their spaciousness and architecture.

Each of the villas, whether located directly on the beach or on the hill, provides panoramic views of the bay and the Andaman Sea. The view is especially beautiful when resting on one of the resort's comfortable loungers. Room interiors are spacious and airy, with white walls and atriums, whose large windows provide for plenty of light. In contrast, the villas' teak floors and wooden wall panels create a sense of visual warmth. Female guests seem to especially appreciate the large bathrooms and dressing rooms.

Thanks to its ideal geographical position, the bay can only be reached via the Chedi or neighbouring Amanpuri. Guests really have

the beach to themselves,
without having to fend off
streams of tourists walking up
and down the sands,
disturbing the peace of the
Chedi's charmed clients.

evason phuket | phuket . thailand

DESIGN: Bernhard Bohnenberger, Sonu + Eva Shivdasani

The Evason Phuket is the second resort in Thailand from Eva Malmström and Sono Shivdasani and, like its sister project in Hua Hin, is still young, as far as its latest reincarnation goes. The hotel's remodelling represents a 180 degree turnaround from what it once was: the Phuket Island Resort, with over 300 rooms, one of the first large-scale resorts on the island. The elongated main building and two further guestroom wings remind one of the banal architecture of the first wave of mass tourism that swept Phuket in the 1970's.

While Malmström and Shivdasani's company, Six Senses, managed the resort, they didn't take long to establish that a drastic change would be required to realize their vision of innovative hospitality. They decided to take over the entire complex, including a portion of the neighbouring isle Bon Island, with its fine sandy beaches.

An ambitious project: "It probably would have been easier to have flattened the whole place, and started again", says the General Manager, Martin Carpenter, but that wasn't possible. And as

with every renovation project, the building threw up its fair share of problems. The drainage system was an example. It emerged that the existing system was simply inadequate for what Eva and Sono had in mind, so a new one had to be constructed. The team not only had to battle against time – they completed the project in just six months – but also with an increasing number of building sites within building sites, that were only kept in check thanks to their talent for improvisation and flexibility. Regardless of setbacks, the fundamental transformation of the ugly

duckling was carried out in record time, although a few more ocean waves will have to crash again the infinity pool wall until the property meets the detailed demands of its owners.

The pool lies directly over the Andaman Sea. Its flat rim gives swimmers the impression of being joined to the ocean. Like the majority of the complex it faces east, nearly on the southernmost point of Phuket, allowing views across the nearby islands. The complex's three restaurants also profit from the panorama, built staggered into a hill that drops

01 | An exemplary renovation of a hotel complex from the 1970's. From the new reception, the view is across the water to nearby islands.

02 | Calming white tones greet guests in the spa centre.

03 | Bedroom in one of the duplex suites. The interior design is certainly functional in the warm, tropical climate.

04 | All duplex suites have open-air bathtubs.

05 | Treatment marquees in the spa area. A meditative place with staggering vistas.

down to the sea. The furthest above is the main restaurant "Into the View", a roofed and walled terrace. Light floor, wall and ceiling colours in beige and white tones, as well as the sleek, reduced furnishings direct your sight to the spectacular natural scenery, which is at its best at 7am, at breakfast.

When the rising sun blinks on the ocean and the fresh morning breeze brings your blood pressure back to a steady level, the coffee and juice tastes three times better, and the day can only go well. At this time of the morning, the buffet is also wonderfully fresh, the light is fantastic and the service relaxed in the

comfortably empty space. In comparison, the "Tree by the Sea" is best visited at lunchtime, for a taste from its pasta and salad buffet, and freshly grilled fish and meats. The 282 completed rooms and duplex suites show a high level of independent design and freshness. They have cool sandstone floors, smooth beige-coloured plaster walls and spacious bathrooms that are just the right answer to the tropical climate. Material combinations, colour choices and furnishings are not just aesthetic, but show that someone with vast travel and hotel experience has taken care of the details. Whether it is the individually designed lights, the bath fittings or the room accessories, the tasteful influence of Eva Malmström is recognizable everywhere.

A central section of the complex is the spa, which is comfortably spread out between palms and bamboo plants next to the restaurants. The Swedish-led team waits with a wide palette of massages and relaxation therapies, including Tai Chi, Qigong or yoga. The treatment rooms in the two-storey building all have views of the ocean, but the "tents" below are infinitely more beautiful, set up on a wooden terrace surrounded by water. A better place to dream is almost impossible to imagine.

04

05

australia

daintree eco lodge | queensland . australia

DESIGN: Terry + Cathy Maloney

Millions of years ago, the earth was largely covered in forest, but around the world today, the last rainforests are in danger. Not just timber production, but also agriculture has destroyed huge areas. Initiatives to protect the green lungs of our planet have sprung up as a result, and are showing positive signs of success. On the east coast of Australia, 12 hectares of forest have been set aside as the Daintree National Park; a 110 million year old treasure chest of plants and animals, representing an entire, intact ecosystem.

In cooperation with the local native Australians, a small hotel complex has been established, allowing visitors a direct experience with this nature, and bringing them closer to the culture of the country's original inhabitants. In the forefront of this project is a respect for the property's unique environment.

Daintree Eco Lodge totals just 15 huts. The idea is not to build an exclusive resort, but to provide a pathway into the forest, without damaging it. The individual huts are constructed on stilts in the thick of the dense vegetation,

and are connected by walkways, allowing the flora and fauna to continue its free rein. The dwellings are simple wooden structures with saddle roofs and large glass doors, giving access to a terrace. The roof's form is visible internally as well, and underscores the natural experience, as does the safari-type style of the interior design. Wooden furniture, beige, brown and green tones, and light, airy fabrics serve to form a fairly clichéed picture. Although the architecture of the huts works in harmony with the elements of the forest, the interior breaks this flow of forms, and

01 | The Daintree Eco Lodge sits in the
     midst of an untouched, intact ecosystem

02 | The individual huts sit on stilts in dense
     rainforest.

02

03 | 04

05

03 | On the 12 hectare site the hotel even
has its "own" waterfall.

04 | Bathing among the ancient trees.

05 | View across the pond to the restaurant.
It serves good, healthy Australian
fusion cuisine.

06 | The spa is small but counts among the
best in Australia. The hotel markets its
own bodycare products under the
Daintree label.

07 | The design of the guestrooms is slick
and functional – a little more innovation
would have a dramatic effect on the
whole complex.

has an almost bourgois effect. The rainforest begins at the door, however, and guests cannot escape its sounds, colours and aromas. In the morning, one is woken by the cry of parrots and in the evening, the gentle murmurs of slumbering monkeys bring guests to rest. Some suites even provide their visitors the chance to bathe with this backdrop, in a jacuzzi on the terrace.

The entire complex is geared up towards an intensive natural experience, from the cuisine full of exotic fruits, nuts, roots and fish from the region, through to the incredible wellness centre and the lodge's special events. Guests can take excursions into the surrounding areas and, under the guidance of native Australians, observe rare birds, or learn about the animals and plants of the nearby Great Barrier Reef.

A waterfall near the resort supplies water for the covered swimming pool which, with its joining sun-terrace, invites for a relaxing afternoon in the tropical, damp heat. The pure, tingly spring water also plays an important role at the wellness centre. Here one can savour a range of underwater massages, mud treatments and face masks, made with natural herbs and roots from the immediate area. The holistic experience of almost untouched nature is an integral part of the concept, and the culture, knowledge and hospitality of Australia's original inhabitants is crucial to this.

lizard island resort | queensland . australia

DESIGN: Desmond Brooks, Stuart Shakespeare, Susan Rossi

When the first European, James Cook, landed on Lizard Island in 1770, he found it difficult to leave again. Admittedly, the reasons for this were of a more technical nature: shallow water and what appeared to be a practically impenetrably large labyrinthine coral reef barred the ship's passage for a long time. But the sufferings of the first intruders on this island were limited. The bountiful tropical fruits, exotic scenery, and crystal-clear water with sandy beaches most certainly made Cook's stay, and that of and his men, infinitely tolerable.

For centuries the island remained an unspoilt natural paradise. It wasn't until the 60s that the first research station was set up. The Lizard Island Resort was added much later. This offers its guests an attraction that in itself may well be classed as unique. Only a few steps away from the beach huts, the bizarre magic of the endless Great Barrier Reef waits beneath the turquoise-coloured water. Diving into these waters means embarking on an impressive journey of discovery with colourful shoals of fish.

The resort provides an exclusive backdrop for this "play" in the form of a back-to-nature holiday location. In the year 2000 it underwent complete renovation, and since then the exterior has been characterised by post-modern chic. In their treatment of colour and structure, the architects around Desmond Brooks and the designer Susan Rossi kept to the surrounding guidelines of rocks, ocean and bush terrain. Following this, the differently sized beach huts are elegant interpretations of typical Queensland houses, with elements made of driftwood as well as fine beech. No aspect of luxury has been left out, as is generally to be expected of a resort of this kind. "Lounging on Lizard" is the principle here

01

01 | From the distance, the construction looks like a landed UFO.
Its open plan and terraces make it one of the most popular
and exclusive properties on the Great Barrier Reef.

02
03

of a relaxed beach life, whether on the veranda of one's own private lodge, at magnificent viewing areas during breathtaking sunsets, or on picnics on remote beaches.

From morning to late evening on the large veranda of the main lodge, an equally elegant Pacific cuisine with excellent Australian wines awaits the resort guests, numbering a maximum of 80. Worth a special mention is the Pavillion Spa with its ancient secret and modern treatments for body and soul. In addition, there are many more adventure activities on the programme other than

diving: sky-diving, for example, or tours of the island through the rainforest. The resort's management places great value on lasting impressions. Whoever visits Lizard Island will feel an echo reverberating within them for a long time to come.

02 | Airy, light and spacious. The resort's rooms are mainly furnished with natural fabrics and materials.

03 | Thanks to the extensive glazing, interior spaces are filled with natural light.

04 | A typical wooden terrace with seaview.

04

south sea

01 | In the Fiji islands, Richard Evanson has realized his own personal dream; a luxurious Crusoe adventure with 14 pavillions.

turtle island | fiji . south sea

DESIGN: Richard Evanson

Conversions and changes of fortune always make interesting stories, and Richard Evanson's tale is certainly a mixed one. Successful in business and incredibly rich he was unhappy, and unfulfiled. The result: alcoholism, a paunch and a personal crisis. Turtle Island turned out to be the answer; one of the many scattered Fijian islands, a tiny piece of paradise on Earth. He bought it, rejuvenated the natural environment that had been totally destroyed by furious cyclones, and set up Turtle Island Resort.

Today, this pint-sized Fijian isle is a breathtaking exotic natural garden. Surrounded by reefs, perfect for diving down into a wonderland inhabited by coral fish, lapped by the crystal-clear waters of the South Pacific and blessed with tiny bays, it is a dream of an island, far away from the western world with its stressful lifestyle. "True to Fijian tradition, on Turtle we live for the moment...not for yesterday or tomorrow, but for today", says Richard Evanson, in a tone that gives away a very personal philosophy, learned the hard way.

The resort in a legendary blue lagoon comprises 14 "bures", as the little houses in Fiji are called. Tropical residences for two, surrounded by palm trees and vegetation, each house has its own sandy bay, waiting right in front of its entrance door that is never locked. Inside, the villas have no ceilings; instead, your eyes will be drawn to the elaborately woven palm roof above. All the bures have exclusive furnishings; luxury-category villas even have a private jacuzzi spa, whilst retaining the typical Fijian style. Trees stripped of their bark act as load-bearing pillars, storage supports, and table legs, with many of the fittings shaped

02

02 | The interior design expresses the island's laid-back
atmosphere.

03 | Tree trunks are employed in the four-poster beds,
as shelving supports and even as table legs.

04 | A picture of island life.

03 04   05

from the same rustic material. Encircled by high white drapes, the kingsize beds are the most intimate, romantic place imaginable. Just lounge and enjoy the sheer indulgence.

And that is the nature of your stay on Turtle Island. Forget all about time and let yourself be pampered - in a group or as a twosome - with exclusive cuisine and an outstanding wine cellar. For couples wishing to embark on the joys of married bliss, enchanting traditional ceremonies are available in caves and on "bili-bili" boats. There are excursions through the island's flora and fauna and endless sporting opportunities just a few steps away. Or you can just lie back in a hammock on the verandah, a book by your side, and let your gaze wander out over the sparkling waters towards the horizon. Put out your hand and reach for your glass, "Darling, would you pour me a little more champagne?".

01 | The yellow-white cement is a fitting material for the region. In skilled combination with wood, stone, grass and textiles, it offers a warm optical effect.

vatulele island resort | fiji . south sea

DESIGN: Martin Livingston, Henry Crawford

The last flight takes 25 minutes, in a small plane, 18 people maximum. The machine scarely leaves the ground, gliding above the Pacific at a perfect height for viewing the seascape. The water becomes more iridescent the closer you get to your final destination. White crests of spray, deep blue sea interwoven with shimmering turquoise. Palm trees appear, a glistening beach and a scattering of huts with palm-frond roofs shaped like pointed caps. On landing,

the single-engine plane flies over the jungle, almost brushing the tops of the trees as it touches down on the asphalt corridor in amongst the tropical vegetation. A tiny piece of paradise which, from above, looks like a sandy footprint.

Vatulele Island Resort is an unadulterated sanctuary. Far away from western civilisation and its tyranny of urgency, immerse yourself in a world still in its natural state. Money is not an issue, but you do have to

have it, and be able to do without the telephone, newspapers, television, radio and other shackles of modern living.

In 1990, Australian film producer Henry Crawford and Fijian Martin Livingston created on Vatulele a scenario that could be a film set in the romantic Robinson Crusoe style. In a sweeping bay with a lagoon just offshore are 18 individual villas standing in isolation, equipped with every conceivable luxury, their own

terrace and own beach. Rooms are generous without exception and a wealth of handmade details emulate the customs of these tiny Fijian islands' native inhabitants. Wild tree stumps are incorporated into the architecture; ceiling paintings take up the organic shapes. Textiles, rugs and bamboo work all tell of the men and the myths of this island world. Fijians' hospitality is legendary; the people looking after you will provide all the little touches that

02 03

make your stay a real pleasure. A whole host of sporting activities awaits and diving, in particular, opens up a fabulous, multicoloured ocean world, all included in the price.

It is a price which is certainly not within everyone's reach, but those who do come here, to escape from civilisation, delight in this world of "barefoot chic", where ties and that little black dress can stay safely in the mirrored wardrobe at home. You don't even need shoes to stroll across the beach to dinner in the evenings. Caribbean/Asian cuisine - all the delicacies of Neptune's kingdom - is served around a large table in the main building. It goes without saying that a romantic table for two is another option.

02 | The ancient trees have simply been incorporated into the buildings.

03 | A good example of how organic and geometric forms can be harmoniously brought together.

04 | **05** Vatulele offers a total of 18 villas, spread across the island. All have terraces that provide wonderful vistas, and have direct access to the beach.

04
05

01 | A total of 14 "bures" await guests on the 22-kilometre-long island.

02 | Quiet, orderly rooms in a fascinating environment.

03 | Most time is normally spent under the shade of a palm tree on the sand, on one of the wooden terraces.

yasawa island resort | fiji . south sea

DESIGN: Garth Downey

The island spans over 22 kilometres, from its northernmost to its southernmost tip, as if stretched out lazily in the Pacific Ocean. Long but narrow, measuring scarcely 1000 metres across at its widest point. From the sky, two smaller islands peeking out from the southern end give Yasawa Island the appearance of an exclamation mark. One of these islands achieved international fame - this is where the film "The Blue Lagoon" was set and from where its title originates.

From the ground, an amazing world awaits guests. Colourful and original, to a large extent undeveloped, and for this reason unspoilt. Quite simply different from the Western world of concrete and roads

and, above all, of endless appointments. A seclusion which sets the Yasawa Island Resort apart from the popular high-life hot spots and distinguishes it as an exceptionally peaceful place.

On Yasawa your footprints could well be the only ones seen in the fine, powdery sand for days. The countless bays provide an inexhaustible reservoir for days of retreat. Ideal for romantic picnics and rendezvous'. The resort offers, in addition, 14 luxury beach villas, each one set in its own private bay. With their thick, sun-bleached thatched roofs and white stone walls, the bures have the appearance of hidden residences, surrounded by entire groves of shady palm trees. Inside, the remarkably

spacious, open rooms merge into one another, similar to within a maisonette. From the terrace, the sleeping area and bathroom are reached via the lounge or living area, all on different levels. The furnishings themselves are well-chosen and stylish, featuring regional touches, that avoid sterotypical kitsch. The atmosphere is determined by a clear, modern design.

Particular objects of desire include the west-facing Lomolagi bures. From here every evening one can witness the amazing spectacle of a sunset flooded sky, just as the diving and snorkelling on offer open up a private galaxy beneath the surface of the water. The all-inclusive rate also includes trips to the Blue

Lagoon caves, adventure tours through the island's rainforest, or a visit to a "lovo", the traditional dance festival held by the local inhabitants. Yasawa Island is a chilled-out journey of discovery in an exotic world where "less is more than enough".

hotel summary

Country	City	Address	Information	Architecture & Design	Page
India	Agra	Amarvilas Taj East Gate Road Agra 282001 India http://www.oberoihotels.com	opened 2001 112 rooms, suites and Kohinoor Suite asian and indian restaurant, bar fitness centre, tennis court, swimming pool, jacuzzi and spa conference facilities for up to 150 people, library 600m away from Taj Mahal	Bensley Design Studio, Bangkok	12
India	Goa	Nilaya Hermitage Arpora Bhati Goa 403518 India http://www.nilayahermitage.com	opened 1994 12 unique guest rooms restaurant and poolside bar tennis court and pool, health club offering Ayurvedic therapies including steam bath, massage, yoga and meditation 1 hour by car to Goa airport	Dean D'Cruz Claudia Derain Hari Ajwani	14
India	Jaipur	Rajvilas Goner Road, Jaipur Rajasthan 303012 India http://www.oberoihotels.com	opened 1997 54 deluxe rooms, 13 luxury tents, 1 royal villa spa, swimming pool and jacuzzi, tennis court business centre and meeting rooms outdoor activities, elephant safaris 8 km from Jaipur centre	Bensley Design Studio, Bangkok	20
India	Uttaranchal	Ananda in the Himalayas NarendraNagar, Dist. Tehri-Garhwal Uttaranchal 249175 India http://www.anandaspa.com	opened 2000 75 deluxe rooms and suites several restaurants spa facilities for body and mind, outdoor facilities conference facilities up to 150 people situated 260km north of Delhi	Mr. Chandu Chhada Chhada Siembieda & Associates	24
India	Udaipur	Devi Garh P.O. Box 144 Udaipur 313001 India http://www.deviresorts.com	opened 2000 23 suites and 7 shikar marquees restaurant and bar fitness centre, steam bath and sauna, massage conference room for up to 45 people 27km north of Udaipur	Gautam Bhatia Navin Gupta Rajv Saini Poddar Family	28

Country	City	Address	Information	Architecture & Design	Page
Indonesia	Bali	Amankila P.O Box 34 80871 Manggis, Karangasem Bali, Indonesia http://www.amankila.com	opened 1993 35 luxury suites, 8 of them with private swimming pool 2 restaurants, bar, beach club with own restaurant library, gallery 3 cascade swimming pools, pool at the beach located in the south-east of Bali, near the village Padang Bai	Edward Tuttle	34
Indonesia	Bali	The Balé P.O Box 76 80363 Nusa Dua Bali, Indonesia http://www.thebale-bali.com	opened 2001 20 pavillions located on a hill, overlooking the Indian Ocean individual pools and verandahs gourmet restaurant, boardroom for up to 18 people private spa, gymnasium, swimming pool, private beach club located right above the Nusa Dua area, in the south of Bali	Antony Lui Karl Princic	40
Indonesia	Bali	Begawan Giri Estate Banjar Begawan Dusun Melinggih Kelod 80571 Ubud Bali, Indonesia http://www.begawan.com	opened 1999 3 four-suite residences, 2 five-suite residences each with a living and dining pavillion, private pool inclusive 2 restaurants, bar, library, amphitheatre beauty treatments and spa facilities	Cheon Yew Kuan Terry Fripp Ratina Huliono Debbie and Bradley Gardner	44
Indonesia	Bali	The Chedi Ubud Desa Melinggih Kelod Payangam, Gianyan 80572 Bali, Indonesia http://www.chediubud.com	opened 1997 54 deluxe rooms, 4 suites restaurant, bar swimming pool, health centre, library, chemist, boutique meeting room for up to 30 people located at the Ayung River, 15 minutes from Ubud	Kerry Hill Architects	48
Indonesia	Bali	Four Seasons Bali at Sayan Sayan - Ubud 80571 Gianyar Bali, Indonesia http://www.fourseasons.com	opened 1998 13 terrace suites, 5 deluxe suites, 28 villas with private pools swimming pool, spa, wellness and fitness centre conference rooms for up to 30 people Ayung Terrace Restaurant, Riverside Cafe, Jati Bar 10 minutes from Ubud	John Heah	52

hotel summary

Country	City	Address	Information	Architecture & Design	Page
Indonesia	Bali	The Legian Jalan Laksmana Seminyak Kuta 80361 Bali, Indonesia http://www.ghmhotels.com	opened 1997 67 suites and 10 Legian Club Villas brasserie style restaurant, pool bar meeting room for up to 30 people, library, boutique swimming pool, beach access, spa and massage located on Bali's west coast, north of Kuta	Jaya Ibrahim Jaya & Associates	58
Indonesia	Bintan	Banyan Tree Bintan Site A4, Lagoi Bintan Island Indonesia http://www.banyantree.com	opened 1995 55 villas distributed over the entire site 3 restaurants and in-villa dining several pools, several watersport facilities, 2 tennis courts, spa on the north-western tip of Bintan island	Ho Kwon Cjan Architrave Design and Planning	62
Malaysia	Langkawi	The Datai Jalan Teluk Datai 07000 Pulau Langkawi Kedah Darul Aman Malaysia http://www.ghmhotels.com	opened 1994 54 deluxe rooms, 18 suites, 40 villas 3 restaurants, bar, beach club health centre, spa, 2 pools, 2 tennis courts, golf course conference room for up to 50 people, library located on the north western coast, 30 minutes to the airport	Kerry Hill Architects	68
Malaysia	Lumut	Pangkor Laut Estates Pangkor Laut Island 32200 Lumut, Perak Malaysia http://www.pangkorlautestates.com	opened 2000 128 villas evenly distributed over the Royal Bay various restaurants and lounges conference rooms for up to 150 people 3 tennis courts, 2 pools, spa and gymnasium	Baldip Singh Bullar YTL Design Group	72
Maldives	Lhaviyani Atoll	Kanuhura Resort Lhaviyani Atoll Maldives http://www.kanuhura.com	opened 2000 102 beach- and sea villas, and suites Thin Rah und Olive Tree Restaurant, 3 bars, disco, Havana Club and Lava Lounge Kanuhura Spa with 9 spa-pavillions, hydrotherapy, massages and gymnasium	Tecton Architects, Malé	76

Country	City	Address	Information	Architecture & Design	Page
Maldives	Vabbinfaru	Banyan Tree Maldives Vabbinfaru Island North Malé Atoll Maldives http://www.banyantree.com	opened 1995 48 villas several restaurants Banyan Tree Spa with jacuzzi and pavillions situated across a small atoll in the Indian Ocean	Ho Kwon Cjan Architrave Design and Planning	80
Maldives	Kuda Huraa	Four Seasons Kuda Huraa North Malé Atoll Maldives http://www.fourseasons.com	opened 1996 106 bungalows and villas, including 38 water bungalows and 26 beach bungalows several restaurants, cafe and bars spa area and gym situated on the island of Kuda Huraa, 30 minutes to the airport	Ground Kent Architects Anke Zieck	82
Maldives	Langkanfushi	Soneva Gili c/o Promus Private Limited 2nd Floor, 4/3 Faamudheyri Magu Malé, Maldives http://www.six-senses.com	opened 2002 29 villa suites, 15 residences gourmet restaurant, villa dining, bar pool, library, tennis courts health spa, watersport facilities situated on the Lankantushi Island, 15 minutes to the airport	Eva and Sonu Shivdasani	86
Maldives	Kunfunadhoo	Soneva Fushi Kunfunadhoo Island Baa Atoll Maldives http://www.six-senses.com	opened 1995 62 villas 3 restaurants, beach barbeque, 2 bars diving school, 2 tennis courts Six Senses Spa with 8 therapy rooms 3 of them with direct seaview	Dick Wells, Tebott & Wells Riyan Design Dick Ismael Rasheed	90
Taiwan	Sun Moon Lake	The Lalu No. 142 Jungshing Road Yuchr, Shiang, Nantou Taiwan 555, R.O.C. http://www.ghmhotels.com	opened 2002 96 guestrooms, suites and villas including a Presidential Suite 2 restaurants, bar, lounge and chinese teahouse spa, gym, sauna and steam, beauty salon, pool, tennis court nearby golf course, boutique, library, several conference rooms located in the heart of central Taiwan near the Sun Moon Lake	Kerry Hill	96

hotel summary

Country	City	Address	Information	Architecture & Design	Page
Thailand	Bangkok	Sukhothai 13/3 South Sathorn Road 10120 Bangkok Thailand http://www.sukhothai.com	opened 1991 146 guestrooms and 78 suites 3 restaurants, The Bar, lobby salons and 2 dining rooms business centre for up to 300 people, private offices pool, gymnasium, sauna, massage located in Bangkok's diplomatic and banking district	Edward Tuttle	102
Thailand	Chiang Mai	Regent Chiang Mai Resort & Spa Mai Rim-Samoeng Old Road 50180 Mai Rim, Chiang Mai Thailand http://www.regenthotels.com	opened 1995 77 suites, built as a traditional "Lanna" village Restaurant Sala Mae Rim, Elephant Bar, pavillion dining pool terrace and bar, library, Lanna Spa tennis court, golf course, boutique located in the north of Thailand, 17km to Chiang Mai	Chulathat Kitibutr Abacus Design Bensley Design	106
Thailand	Hua Hin	Chiva Som 73/4 Petchkasem Road 77110 Hua Hin Thailand http://www.chivasom.com	opened 2001 33 rooms and 7 suites with seaview, 17 Thai pavillions The Emerald Room, Waves, Orchid Lounge, piano lounge many offers around spa, massage, beauty salon, pool library, 2 small meeting rooms ro up to 25 people, boutique located in the east of Thailand, near the King's summer palace	Jean-Paul Blissett Syntax Group	112
Thailand	Hua Hin	Evason Hua Hin 9 Parknampran Beach Prachuab Khiri Khan, 77220 Thailand http://www.six-senses.com	opened 2002 182 rooms 3 restaurants swimming pool, golf course, tennis court, spa area 2 function and conference centres located at Pranburi, a short 20 minute drive to Hua Hin town	Bernhard Bohnenberger Eva and Sonu Shivdasani	114
Thailand	Koh Samui	Muang Kulaypan 100 Moo 2, T. Bophut Koh Samui, Suratthani 8432 Thailand www.sawadee.com/samui/kulaypan	opened 1996 41 guestrooms, including 7 honeymoon suites and 1 VIP Suite Budsaba Restaurant and Kula Bar pool, reading room and tour service 10 minutes to Koh Samui Airport	M.L. Archava Varavana	120

Country	City	Address	Information	Architecture & Design	Page
Thailand	Phuket	Amanpuri Pansea Beach Phuket Island Thailand http://www.amanpuri.com	opened 1988 40 thai style pavillions and 30 villas restaurant and bar pool, spa facilities, gym, library, golf and tennis on the west coast of Phuket direct on the beach 25 minutes to the Phuket airport	Edward Tuttle	122
Thailand	Phuket	Banyan Tree Phuket 34 Moo 4, Srisoonthorn Road Chrengtalay 83110 Phuket Thailand http://www.banyantree.com	opened 1994 109 mansions, many with pool golf course, wellness and beauty farm 3 meeting rooms for 18, 63 and 100 people 15 km to the south of Phuket Airport	Ho Kwon Cjan Architrave Design and Planning	126
Thailand	Phuket	The Chedi Phuket Pansea Bay, 118 Moo 3 Choeng Talay Talang District 83110, Phuket Thailand http://www.chedi-phuket.com	re-opened 1995 89 one- and 19 two-bedroom cottages 3 restaurants, bar conference facilities for up to 150 people pool, library, spa, 2 tennis courts, water sports near Patong Beach, 25 minute drive to the airport in Phuket	Edward Tuttle Jon Vorapot Somton	130
Thailand	Phuket	Evason Phuket 100 Vised Road, Moo 2 Tambon Rawai 83130 Muang District, Phuket Thailand http://www.six-senses.com	opened 2001 281 rooms in different categories 4 bars 3 pools, 2 volleyball courts, fitness centre dive school, health spa, several conterence rooms private beach on Bon Island exclusive to resort guests	Bernhard Bohnenberger Eva and Sonu Shivdasani	134
Australia	Queensland	Daintree Eco Lodge 21 Daintree Road 4873 Daintree, Queensland Australia www.daintree-ecolodge.com.au	re-opened 1995 150 rainforest villas gourmet dining spa, pure spring water near to the Daintree National Park, 90 minutes to Cairns	Cathy and Terry Maloney	140

hotel summary

Country	City	Address	Information	Architecture & Design	Page
Australia	Queensland	Lizard Island Resort P.M.B. 40 4870 Lizard Island, Queensland Australia www.lizardisland-australia.com	opened 2001 total of 40 rooms, including 18 beach suites and 16 villas restaurant, Ospreys Restaurant, bar and lounge Pavillion Spa, beach club, tennis court, gymnasium conference rooms located in a national park with sandy beaches and a lagoon	Desmond Brooks Susan Rossi	144
Fiji	Turtle Island	Turtle Island C/- Turtle Island Holidays Ground Floor, 411 Collins Street Melbourne. Vic 3000 Australia http://www.turtlefiji.com	re-opened 2000 14 huts jacuzzi exclusive cuisine with extensive wine cellar located directly on a natural lagoon	Richard Evanson	150
Fiji	Vatulele Island	Vatulele Island Resort Vatulele Island Fiji http://www.vatulele.com	re-opened 2002 18 villas dive school Vatulele is a 25 minute flight by light aircraft from Nadi International Airport	Martin Livingston Henry Crawford	154
Fiji	Yasawa Island	Yasawa Island Resort P.O. Box 10128 Nadi Airport Fiji http://www.yasawaislandresort.com	re-opened 2001 15 bures restaurant, Bure Levu lounge and bar pool and tennis court dive school situated directly on the beach, 35 minutes to Nadi airport	Garth Downey	158

architects & designers

photo credits

all other photos by:

Roland Bauer and Martin N. Kunz

imprint

Die Deutsche Bibliothek – CIP Data

Best designed wellness hotels /
Martin Nicholas Kunz. - Ludwigsburg : av-Ed.

1. India, Far East, Australia, South Pacific. - 2002

ISBN 3-929638-91-6

Printed in Germany

lebensart global networks AG
Konrad-Adenauer-Allee 35 | 86150 Augsburg | Germany
p +49-821-34545928 | f +49-821-34545925
http://www.lebensart-ag.com | publishing@lebensart-ag.com

avedition
Königsallee 57 | 71638 Ludwigsburg | Germany
p +49-7141-1477391 | f +49-7141-1477399
http://www.avedition.de | info@avedition.de

Publisher | Martin Nicholas Kunz
Texts (page) | Sybille Eck (10), Bärbel Holzberg (82),
Ina Sinterhauf (40, 62, 80, 86, 138), Heinfried Tacke (96, 112,
144, 150, 154, 158) All other texts by Martin Nicholas Kunz and
Scott M. Crouch
Translations & Editing | Nigel Geens (12, 62, 80, 82, 86, 150,
154), Vineeta Manglani (24, 106, 144, 158), Mathis Martin
(20, 40, 112, 122, 126), all other by Scott M. Crouch
Research | Hanna Martin, Saskia Lang
Art Direction | Willem Krauss, Michael Schickinger
Production | Markus Hartmann, Martina Weißer, Hanna Martin
Druck | Schoder Druck KG, Gersthofen

Special Thanks to:

Hari Ajwani, Nilaya Hermitage | Rolf Berthold, Kanuhura |
Debbie & Bradley Gardner, Begawan Giri Estate |
Martin Carpenter, Evason Phuket | Jamie Case, Datai |
Miriya Chacko, Ananda Himalaya | Ragini Chopra, Oberoi
Hotels & Resorts | Henry Crawford, Vatulele Island Resort |
Claudia Derain; Nilaya | Trina Dingler-Ebert, Amanresorts |
Sesotya Djajadi, Begawan Giri Estate | Andrew Fairley, Turtle
Island | Julia Gajcak, Four Seasons Resort Kuda Huraa |
Julia Gauci, Lizard Island Resort | Neeta Gupta & Poddar
Family, Devi Garh | Guy Heywood, Amankila | Hans R. Jenni,
GHM Hotels & Resorts | Barbara Jensen, Sukhothai |
Amarin Kocharat, Six Senses Hotels & Resorts |
Nicole Kochornswasdi, Chiva Som | André Kretschmann,
Chedi Phuket | John G. Laing, Chedi Ubud | Eva Malmström,
Six Senses Hotels & Resorts | Hansjörg Meier, The Legian |
Zeena Mosa, Banyan Tree Resorts | Trent Munda, Evason
Hua Hin | Laurent A. M. Myter, Pangkor Laut | Marc Ribail,
Muan Kulaypan | Sono Shivdasani, Six Senses Hotels &
Resorts |Kymberley | Sproule, Regent Chiang Mai Resort & Spa
| Mira Szarata, Design Hotels Bali | Rainata Tjoa, The Balé,
Sanctuary Resorts | Larry van Ooyen, The Lalu | Dagmar von
Tschurtschenthaler | Ferdinand Wortelboer, Amanpuri

Martin Nicholas Kunz

Born 1957 in Hollywood.
Martin is Senior Vice
President media of lebensart
global networks AG. Martin
worked as an editor for
several German and other
international magazines such
as "design report" and was
Managing Director of New
Media for the German
publisher DVA. He is author
and co-author of several
design, craft and construction
books.

Other books by Martin
Nicholas Kunz published by
avedition lebensart :
best designed hotels in asia,
australia & new zealand,
best designed hotels in
europe I – urban locations,
best designed hotels in
europe II – countryside,
best designed hotels in north &
south america.